SARVODAYA

Owing to the antiquity and rarity of this book, certain pages are regrettably absent, and readability is compromised due to the blurring of the original text. If you possess any insights regarding the availability of these missing sections, kindly inform us. Your assistance is crucial in ensuring the completion of this significant work for the benefit of future generations.

SARVODAYA

THE WELFARE OF ALL

M. K. GANDHI

GYAN

Published by

GYAN

Gyan Publishing House
5, Ansari Road
Daryaganj, New Delhi-110002
Phone: 011-47034999, 9811692060
E-mail: books@gyanbooks.com

Distribution Network
gyanbooks.com
India, USA, Canada, UK, Australia

ISBN: 978-93-7316-350-5 (PB)

First Published, 1935

2nd Impression 2025

Printed at: Gyan Press, Delhi.

SARVODAYA
Author: M. K. GANDHI

SARVODAYA

(The Welfare of All)

By

M. K. GANDHI

Edited by

BHARATAN KUMARAPPA

NAVAJIVAN PUBLISHING HOUSE
AHMEDABAD

EDITOR'S NOTE

A small brochure entitled *Sarvodaya, Its Principles and Programme* was issued in 1951 by the Navajivan Publishing House at short notice in response to pressing demand. Its chief aim was to give in a few pages information regarding the principles and programme of the Sarvodaya Samaj, which was a fellowship started in Wardha, India, by Gandhiji's followers after his passing away. The present volume deals with Sarvodaya proper, or the welfare of all, and how it may be attained.

Sarvodaya, as the welfare of all, represents the ideal social order according to Gandhiji. Its basis is all-embracing love. So it has room in it for all without exception — prince and peasant, Hindu and Muslim, touchable and untouchable, white and black, saint and sinner. No individual or group is to be suppressed, exploited or liquidated. All are to be equally members of this social order, all sharing in the produce of their labour, the strong protecting the weak and functioning as trustees for the weak, and each promoting the welfare of all.

As one of the essential qualities of love is self-giving, or emptying oneself or dying for the loved one, self-control and self-suffering form one of the prime requisites for realizing Sarvodaya. India with her centuries of renunciation and austere self-control provides thus the best soil for it. In marked contrast is the Western craze for comfort, for multiplication of wants and self-indulgence. Gandhiji set himself in strong opposition to this trend in Western civilization precisely because he knew that it could not lead to Sarvodaya or social justice, but only to greed, conflict, and suppression of the weak by the strong, whether under Capitalism or under Communism.

A philosophy such as this, of all-embracing, self-suffering love, presupposes deep spiritual foundations. It implies a living faith in the One that pervades all. It requires also great self-discipline and training, and development of soul-force. In this its essentially spiritual basis it is the very antithesis of Communism which is avowedly materialistic, although in regard to its goal Sarvodaya is similar to Communism.

Its basis being spiritual, the means for achieving Sarvodaya is also spiritual. Communism holds out the hope that the ideal social order can be realized only when the exploiter is done away with by physical force. For this it builds on class hatred and resorts to periodical purges and war. To Gandhiji, on the other hand, such a method seemed entirely futile, for hatred and violence were bound sooner or later to recoil on their perpetrator, and to produce more hatred and violence in their wake. The way to end oppression, accordingly he believed, was to appeal to the conscience and reason of the oppressor by self-suffering and nobility of character, and to convert him and make him a willing ally of the new social order. The technique he evolved for this purpose, the technique of Satyagraha or clinging to Truth and Non-violence at the cost of untold suffering to oneself and even death, was one of his distinctive contributions, and very central to his teaching.

Gandhiji did not believe in drawing up a futile Utopia. The goal did not interest him more than as a pole star by which to steer his course through the storms which life presented. Not for him the distant scene. He did not therefore trouble to give us a detailed blue-print of the ideal social order. His concern was much rather with the means i.e., with shaping the present in the light of the goal. He was certain that if we could work out our ideal in terms of the immediate present, the end was bound to follow. Accordingly he dealt from the Sarvodaya point of view with various problems as they confronted him from day to day, such as those of Industrialism, Capital and Labour, Landlord and Peasant, treated in this book.

Such an essentially realistic and practical approach on the part of Gandhiji has had an amazingly wholesome effect, for since his death his followers have concerned themselves with going forward in the application of his great principles of Truth and Non-violence to the immediate problems confronting the nation. Of all such problems, the greatest, of course, is the economic one of freeing our people from poverty and want. Gandhiji himself sought to tackle it by trying to revive village industries, a symbol of which was hand-spinning, which occupied the first place in his economic programme. Not that he did not realize the importance of agriculture, but that he felt that with a foreign government at the helm nothing much could be done to improve the lot of the agriculturist, weighed down as he was by tenancy laws and a wooden system of land revenue and village administration. But with the advent of independence, Gandhiji's followers have rightly taken up the problem of land, which is the most crucial for the agriculturist who forms the backbone of our nation.

The principle of love underlying Sarvodaya demands that land, the instrument of production, should not be denied to him who works on it. To refuse land to a cultivator is to refuse him his means of livelihood, and thus to reduce him to a state of helplessness whereby he becomes a victim of exploitation and enslavement. But how is land to be secured for the landless without liquidating the landlord who parasitically lives on the labour of the landless worker?

This was the problem which Acharya Vinoba Bhave, a close associate and disciple of Gandhiji since 1916, set out to tackle in April 1951 in a violence-ridden, Communist area of India. His solution was in accordance with the teachings of Gandhiji. He appealed to the best in the landlord and obtained free gifts of land. Thus was born his great Bhoodan or Land Gifts Mission, which has startled the world by its remarkable success. Already almost 2 million acres of land have been secured for the landless through this means, and it is hoped to attain the goal of 50 million acres for 50 million of India's landless labourers by 1957, so that by that year there will be no landless labour in India. Here is bloodless revolution unprecedented in the history of the world, whereby a step is taken in the direction of Sarvodaya or the ideal social order, by converting the exploiter and making his services still available to society, instead of doing away with him and depriving ourselves of his ability for organization and management.

As this followed by Vinoba's Wealth Gifts Mission (Sampattidan) is an important development out of Gandhiji's Sarvodaya movement, the publishers recently brought out a separate volume, entitled *Bhoodan Yajna* (Land Gifts Mission) by Vinoba Bhave, containing Vinoba's writings and speeches on the subject of Bhoodan and Sampattidan. Consequently we have not included this topic here, although it is necessarily a part of the Sarvodaya movement.

Not content with Land Gifts and Wealth Gifts, Vinoba has recently suggested also Labour Gifts (Shramadan), thus enabling all, and not merely landowners and people with money, but even those who have only labour at their disposal, to partake in this movement of service and sacrifice on behalf of the less privileged.

Besides this practical development, Vinoba and a few other close associates of Gandhiji have carried Gandhiji's thoughts on Sarvodaya a little further, especially in regard to Economic Equality, Body Labour, Non-possession and Planning. A selection from among these is given in Part II of this volume to show how Gandhiji's ideas regarding Sarvodaya are developing. We have also included in this Part the programme being advocated for Sarvodaya workers after Gandhiji's death. We have not included Bhoodan, however, in the programme, although it occupies the foremost attention of Sarvodaya workers today, only because it is covered by the volume devoted to the subject of Bhoodan already referred to.

For the convenience of the reader we have selected out of Gandhiji's writings and speeches for over thirty years, only such passages as represent the distinctive aspects of his teaching on Sarvodaya. This forms Part I or the major part of the present volume. For further elaboration of his views, the interested reader should see other books by Gandhiji such as *Towards Non-violent Socialism, Rebuilding our Villages, Constructive Programme, Basic Education, Women and Social Injustice, For Pacifists, Communal Unity,* and *Drink, Drugs and Gambling,* all published by the Navajivan Publishing House, Ahmedabad-9.

Dates are attached to the writings quoted here from the *Young India* and the *Harijan,* Gandhiji's weeklies. In regard to quotations from books by Gandhiji, it may be of interest to know that the *Hind Swaraj* was written in 1908, *From Yeravda Mandir* in 1930, *Unto This Last: A Paraphrase* first published in book-form in Gujarati in 1908 and in English in 1951, and the *Autobiography* in 1927 and 1929. *Gandhiji's Writings and Speeches* was published by Natesan & Co., Madras, first edition in 1917 and fourth edition in 1933.

Sarvodaya may well be regarded as India's distinctive contribution to social philosophy. Its roots go back to almost 3000 years when Buddha and Mahavir went about preaching love or non-violence, and to those ancient seers who through the centuries taught and practised austerity and self-control, and sought to inculcate them in the individual through social institutions such as the joint-family, caste and village organization. In the family, caste and village community life the individual learnt to curb his own desires for the sake of his group, to share his produce with others, to co-operate with them, to feel loyalty to the group and to accept its discipline. He enjoyed economic security as his work and minimum requirements were assured to him by the group. There was a feeling of kinship and equality between him and other members of his group as in a family. It was village communism without Communism's violence. It was from these sources that Gandhiji drew his inspiration for Sarvodaya or the ideal social order, although immediately it was from a reading of Ruskin's *Unto This Last.* Gandhiji was convinced that if individual and social life were not thus based on love and high moral and spiritual principles, no amount of preaching, establishing world organizations for peace, and resisting war will avail, for peace is the end-result of our daily living. Consequently he was at great pains to show, even as our ancestors had done in the past, how the individual and society were to be transformed if we were to progress towards the ideal social order.

The question that faces humanity today is how we may attain peace and freedom for all. Can we obtain them if we pursued the way of self-indulgence and aggressive industrialism with its greed for the world's resources and markets, and if we built up mammoth organizations backed by military might to control others for our own ends, or should we rather go the Gandhian way of simplicity and economically self-sufficient small community-organization, wherein the individual will live for all through service and self-sacrifice ? The two lead in entirely opposite directions. Of this there is no mistaking. One moves inevitably towards hatred, war and destruction, the other is calculated to lead to love, peace and the welfare of all alike. The destiny of man depends on his choice between the two ways. It is high time that both we in India and others stopped to reflect seriously over the issues involved. It is to this end that this book has been compiled. It aims to present the Gandhian way, or what may be described as Gandhiji's gospel of peace, and freedom, for a world torn by strife and ever increasingly haunted by suicidal war and too great centralization of power.

Bombay, September, 1953 Bharatan Kumarappa

CONTENTS

C. Capital and Labour

D. Landlord and Peasant

SECTION FOUR: SOCIAL ORDER

A. The Narrower Society—Man

B. The Larger Society—Animals

SECTION FIVE: POLITICAL ORDER

A. Sarvodaya State

B. Its External Relations

SECTION SIX: RESISTANCE TO EVIL

A. The Method of Satyagraha

B. Economic Inequality

C. Social Disorder

D. Political Evils

SECTION SEVEN: WORKERS AND WORK PROGRAMME

A. The Worker

B. The Programme

SARVODAYA

PART I

By Gandhiji

SECTION ONE: MEANING OF SARVODAYA

1

INTRODUCTORY

During the days of my education I had read practically nothing outside text-books, and after I launched into active life I had very little time for reading. I cannot, therefore, claim much book knowledge. However, I believe I have not lost much because of this enforced restraint. On the contrary, the limited reading may be said to have enabled me thoroughly to digest what I did read. Of these books, the one that brought about an instantaneous and practical transformation in my life was *Unto This Last*. I translated it later into Gujarati, entitling it *Sarvodaya* (the welfare of all).

I believe that I discovered some of my deepest convictions reflected in this great book of Ruskin, and that is why it so captured me and made me transform my life. A poet is one who can call forth the good latent in the human breast. Poets do not influence all alike, for every one is not evolved in an equal measure.

The teachings of *Unto This Last* I understood to be:

1. That the good of the individual is contained in the good of all.

2. That a lawyer's work has the same value as the barber's inasmuch as all have the same right of earning their livelihood from their work.

3. That a life of labour, i.e. the life of the tiller of the soil and the handicraftsman is the life worth living.

The first of these I knew. The second I had dimly realized. The third had never occurred to me. *Unto This Last* made it as clear as daylight for me that the second and the third were contained in the first. I arose with the dawn, ready to reduce these principles to practice.

Autobiography, 1948; pt. IV, ch. XVIII

2

THE GREATEST GOOD OF ALL

A votary of Ahimsa cannot subscribe to the utilitarian formula (of the greatest good of the greatest number). He will strive for the greatest good of all and die in the attempt to realize the idea. He will, therefore, be willing to die, so that the others may live. He will serve himself with the rest, by himself dying. The greatest good of all inevitably includes the good of the greatest number, and therefore, he and the utilitarian will converge in many points in their career, but there does come a time when they must part company, and even work in opposite directions. The utilitarian to be logical will never sacrifice himself. The absolutist will even sacrifice himself.

Young India, 9-12-'26

3

SARVODAYA IN OUTLINE

If we would see our dream of Sarvodaya * i.e. true democracy realized, we would regard the humblest and lowest Indian as being equally the ruler of India with the tallest in the land. This presupposes that all are pure or will become pure if they are not. And purity must go hand-in-hand with wisdom. No one would then harbour any distinction between community and community, caste and outcaste. Everybody would regard all as equal with oneself and hold them together in the silken net of love. No one would regard another as untouchable. We would hold as equal the toiling labourer and the rich capitalist. Everybody would know how to earn an honest living by the sweat of one's brow and make no distinction between

* The term used here is Panchayat Raj, which for Gandhiji meant the same as Sarvodaya. — Ed.

intellectual and physical labour. To hasten this consummation, we would voluntarily turn ourselves into scavengers. No one who has wisdom will ever touch opium, liquor or any intoxicants. Everybody would observe Swadeshi as the rule of life and regard every woman, not being his wife, as his mother, sister or daughter according to her age, never lust after her in his heart. He would be ready to lay down his life when occasion demands it, never want to take another's life.

Harijan, 18-1-'48

SECTION TWO: ITS SPIRITUAL BASIS

A. INTRODUCTORY

1

MEANS ALL IMPORTANT

The clearest possible definition of the goal and its appreciation would fail to take us there, if we do not know and utilize the means of achieving it. I have, therefore, concerned myself principally with the conservation of the means and their progressive use. I know if we can take care of them, attainment of the goal is assured. I feel too that our progress towards the goal will be in exact proportion to the purity of our means.

This method may appear to be long, perhaps too long, but I am convinced that it is the shortest.

Amrit Bazar Patrika, 17-9-'33

2

DUTIES NOT RIGHTS

If all simply insist on rights and no duties, there will be utter confusion and chaos. If instead of insisting on rights every one does his duty, there will immediately be the rule of order established among mankind. If you apply this simple and universal rule to employers and labourers, landlords and tenants, the princes and their subjects, or the Hindus and the Muslims, you will find that the happiest relations can be established in all walks of life without creating disturbance in and dislocation of life and business which you see in India as in the other parts of the world. What I call the law of Satyagraha is to be deduced from an appreciation of duties and rights flowing therefrom.

What, for example, is the duty of the Hindu towards his Muslim neighbour? His duty is to befriend him as a man, to share his joys and sorrows and help him in distress. He will then have the right to expect similar treatment from his Muslim neighbour and will probably get the expected response. But suppose that the few Muslims do not reciprocate the correct behaviour of the many Hindus and show fight in every action, it will be a sign of unmanliness. What is then the duty of the many Hindus? Certainly not to overpower them by the brute strength of the many; that will be usurpation of an unearned right. Their duty will be to check their unmanly behaviour as they would that of their blood-brothers.

Harijan, 6-7-'47

3

MORAL MEANS ESSENTIAL

People in the West generally hold that the whole duty of man is to promote the happiness of the majority of mankind, and happiness is supposed to mean only physical happiness and economic prosperity. If the laws of morality are broken in the conquest of this happiness, it does not matter very much. The consequences of this line of thinking are writ large on the face of Europe.

This exclusive search for physical and economic well-being prosecuted in disregard of morality is contrary to divine law, as some wise men in the West have shown. One of these was John Ruskin who contends in *Unto This Last* that men can be happy only if they obey the moral law.

Morality is an essential ingredient in all the faiths of the world, but apart from religion, our commonsense indicates the necessity of observing the moral law. Only by observing it can we hope to be happy.

(From Gandhiji's Introduction to his paraphrase of Ruskin's *Unto This Last*, 1951; pp. IX–XI).

B. THE VIRTUES REQUIRED

1

TRUTH

All our activities should be centred in Truth. Truth should be the very breath of our life. When once this stage in the pilgrim's progress is reached, all other rules of correct living will come without effort, and obedience to them will be instinctive. But without Truth it is impossible to observe any principles or rules in life.

Truth is the right designation of God. Hence there is nothing wrong in every man following Truth according to his lights. Indeed it is his duty to do so. Then if there is a mistake on the part of any one so following Truth, it will be automatically set right. For the quest of Truth involves Tapas — self-suffering, sometimes even unto death. There can be no place in it for even a trace of self-interest. In such selfless search for Truth nobody can lose his bearings for long. Directly he takes to the wrong path he stumbles, and is thus redirected to the right path.

***From Yeravda Mandir*, 1945; pp. 2-3**

2

NON-VIOLENCE OR LOVE

Ahimsa (non-violence) is not the crude thing it has been made to appear. Not to hurt any living thing is no doubt a part of Ahimsa. But it is its least expression. The principle of Ahimsa is violated by every evil thought, by undue haste, by lying, by hatred, by wishing ill to anybody. It is also violated by our holding on to what the world needs.

Without Ahimsa it is not possible to seek and find Truth. Ahimsa and Truth are so intertwined that it is practically impossible to disentangle and separate them. They are like the two sides of a coin, or rather of a smooth unstamped metallic disc. Who can say, which is the obverse, and which is the reverse? Nevertheless Ahimsa is the means; Truth is the end. Means to be means must always be within our reach, and so Ahimsa is our supreme duty. If we take care of the means, we are bound to reach the end sooner or later. When once we have grasped this point, final victory is beyond question.

From Yeravda Mandir, 1945; pp. 7–9

When non-violence is accepted as the law of life it must pervade the whole being and not be applied to isolated acts. It is a profound error to suppose that whilst the law is good enough for individuals it is not for masses of mankind.

Harijan, 5-9-'36

If we turn our eyes to the time of which history has any record down to our own time, we shall find that man has been steadily progressing towards Ahimsa. Our remote ancestors were cannibals. Then came a time when they were fed up with cannibalism and they began to live on chase. Next came a stage when man was ashamed of leading the life of a wandering hunter. He therefore took to agriculture and depended principally on mother earth for his food. Thus from being a nomad he settled down to civilized stable life, founded villages and towns, and from member of a family he became member of a community and a nation. All these are signs of progressive Ahimsa and diminishing Himsa. Had it been otherwise, the human species should have been extinct by now even as many of the lower species have disappeared.

Prophets and Avatars have also taught the lesson of Ahimsa more or less. Not one of them has professed to teach Himsa. And how should it be otherwise? Himsa does not need to be taught. Man as animal is violent, but as Spirit is non-violent. The moment he awakes to the Spirit within he cannot remain violent. Either he progresses towards Ahimsa or rushes to his doom. That is why the prophets and Avatars have taught the lessons of truth, harmony, brotherhood, justice, etc. — all attributes of Ahimsa.

If we believe that mankind has steadily progressed towards Ahimsa, it follows that it has to progress towards it still further. Nothing in this world is static, everything is kinetic. If there is no progression, then there is inevitable retrogression.

Harijan, 11-8-'40

3

BRAHMACHARYA OR CHASTITY

Now for the definition — the meaning — of Brahmacharya. Its root meaning may be given thus : that conduct which puts one in touch with God.

The conduct consists in the fullest control over all the senses. This is the true and relevant meaning of the word.

Popularly it has come to mean mere physical control over the organ of generation. This narrow meaning has debased Brahmacharya and made its practice all but impossible. Control over the organ of generation is impossible without proper control over all the senses. They are all interdependent. Mind on the lower plane is included in the senses. Without control over the mind mere physical control, even if it can be attained for a time, is of little or no use.

Harijan, 13-6-'36

Control of the palate is very closely connected with the observance of Brahmacharya. I have found from experience that the observance of celibacy becomes comparatively easy, if one acquires mastery over the palate.

From Yeravda Mandir, 1945; p. 15

If a man gives his love to one woman, or a woman to one man, what is there left for all the world besides? It simply means, "We two first, and the devil take all the rest of them." As a faithful wife must be prepared to sacrifice her all for the sake of her husband, and a faithful husband for the sake of his wife, it is clear that such persons cannot rise to the height of universal love, or look upon all mankind as kith and kin. For they have created a boundary wall round their love. The larger their family, the farther are they from universal love. Hence one who would obey the law of Ahimsa cannot marry, not to speak of gratification outside the marital bond.

Then what about people who are already married? Will they never be able to realize Truth? Can they never offer up their all at the altar of humanity? There is a way out for them. They can behave as if they were not married. Those who have enjoyed this happy condition will be able to bear me out. Many have to my knowledge successfully tried the experiment. If the married couple can think of each other as brother and sister, they are freed for universal service. The very thought that all the women in the world are his sisters, mothers or daughters will at once ennoble a man and snap his chains. The husband and wife do not lose anything here, but only add to their resources and even to their family. Their love becomes free from the impurity of lust and so grows stronger.

From Yeravda Mandir, 1945; pp. 10, 11

4

FEARLESSNESS

Fearlessness is indispensable for the growth of the other noble qualities. How can one seek Truth, or cherish Love, without Fearlessness? As Pritam says, 'The path of Hari (the Lord) is the path of the brave, not of cowards.' Hari here means Truth, and the brave are those armed with Fearlessness.

From Yeravda Mandir, 1945; p. 27

5

NON-STEALING

It is impossible that a person should steal, and simultaneously claim to know Truth or cherish Love. Yet every one of us is consciously or unconsciously more or less guilty of theft. It is theft to take something in the belief that it is nobody's property. Things found on the roadside belong to the ruler or the local authority.

It is theft to take something from another even with his permission if we have no real need of it. We should not receive any single thing that we do not need. Theft of this description generally has food for its object. It is theft for me to take any fruit that I do not need, or to take it in a larger quantity than is necessary. We are not always aware of our real needs, and most of us improperly multiply our wants, and thus unconsciously make thieves of ourselves. If we devote some thought to the subject, we shall find that we can get rid of quite a number of our wants. One who follows the observance of Non-stealing will bring about a progressive reduction of his own wants. Much of the distressing poverty in this world has arisen out of breaches of the principle of Non-stealing.

One, who observes the principle of Non-stealing, will refuse to bother himself about things to be acquired in the future. This evil anxiety for the future will be found at the root of many a theft. Today we only desire possession of a thing; tomorrow we shall begin to adopt measures, straight if possible, crooked when thought necessary, to acquire its possession.

Ideas may be stolen no less than material things. One who egoistically claims to have originated some good idea, which, really speaking, did not originate with him, is guilty of a theft of ideas.

One who takes up the observance of Non-stealing has therefore to be humble, thoughtful, vigilant and in habits simple.

From Yeravda Mandir, 1945; pp. 19–22

6

NON-POSSESSION

Non-possession is allied to Non-stealing. A thing not originally stolen must nevertheless be classified as stolen property, if we possess it without needing it. Possession implies provision for the future. A seeker after Truth, a follower of the law of Love cannot hold anything against tomorrow. God never stores for the morrow; He never creates more than what is strictly needed for the moment. If therefore we repose faith in His providence, we should rest assured that He will give us every day our daily bread, meaning everything that we require. Saints and devotees, who have lived in such faith, have always derived a justification for it from their experience. Our ignorance or negligence of the Divine Law, which gives to man from day to day his daily bread and no more, has given rise to inequalities with all the miseries attendant upon them. The rich have a superfluous store of things which they do not need, and which are therefore neglected and wasted; while millions are starved to death for want of sustenance. If each retained possession only of what he needed, no one would be in want, and all would live in contentment. As it is, the rich are discontented no less than the poor. The poor man would fain become a millionaire, and the millionaire a multimillionaire. The rich should take the initiative in dispossession with a view to a universal diffusion of the spirit of contentment. If only they keep their own property within moderate limits, the starving will be easily fed, and will learn the lesson of contentment along with the rich.

From the standpoint of pure Truth, the body too is a possession. We thus arrive at the ideal of total renunciation, and learn to use the body for the purposes of service so long as it exists, so much so that service, and not bread, becomes with us the staff of life. We eat and drink, sleep and wake, for service alone. Such an attitude of mind brings us real happiness.

From Yeravda Mandir, 1945; pp. 23–25

Nature produces enough for our wants from day to day, and if only everybody took enough for himself and nothing more, there would be no pauperism in this world, there would be no man dying of starvation in this world. But so long as we have got this inequality, so long we are thieving. I am no Socialist and I do not want to dispossess those who have got possessions; but I do say that, personally, those of us who want to see light out of darkness have to follow this rule. I do not want to dispossess anybody. I should then be departing from the rule of Ahimsa. If somebody else possesses more than I do, let him. But so far as my own life has to be regulated, I do say that I dare not possess anything which I do not want. In India we have got three millions of people having to be satisfied with one meal a day, and that meal consisting of a Chapati containing no fat in it, and a pinch of salt. You and I have really no right to anything that we have until these three millions are clothed and fed better. You and I, who ought to know better, must adjust our wants, and even undergo voluntary starvation in order that they may be nursed, fed and clothed.

Speeches and Writings of Mahatma Gandhi, 4th Ed., p. 384

7

RESTRAINT IN FOOD AND DRINK

Abstemiousness from intoxicating drinks and drugs, and from all kinds of foods, especially meat, is undoubtedly a great aid to the evolution of the spirit, but it is by no means an end in itself. Many a man eating meat and with everybody but living in the fear of God is nearer his freedom than a man religiously abstaining from meat and many other things but blaspheming God in every one of his acts.

Young India, 6-10-'21

I do feel that spiritual progress does demand at some stage that we should cease to kill our fellow creatures for the satisfaction of our bodily wants. The beautiful lines of Goldsmith occur to me as I tell you of my vegetarian fad :

No flocks that range the valley free
To slaughter I condemn,
Taught by the Power that pities me
I learn to pity them.

India's Case for Swaraj, 1932. p. 402

Experience teaches that animal food is unsuited to those who would curb their passions. But it is wrong to overestimate the importance of food in the formation of character or in subjugating the flesh. Diet is a powerful factor not to be neglected. But to sum up all religion in terms of diet, as is often done in India, is as wrong as it is to disregard all restraint in regard to diet and to give full reins to one's appetite.

Young India, 7-10-'26

Ahimsa is not a mere matter of dietetics, it transcends it. What a man eats or drinks matters little ; it is the self-denial, the self-restraint behind it that matters. By all means practise as much restraint in the choice of the articles of your diet as you like. The restraint is commendable, even necessary, but it touches only the fringe of Ahimsa. A man may allow himself a wide latitude in the matter of diet and yet may be a personification of Ahimsa and compel our homage, if his heart overflows with love and melts at another's woe, and has been purged of all passions. On the other hand, a man always overscrupulous in diet is an utter stranger to Ahimsa and a pitiful wretch if he is a slave to selfishness and passions and is hard of heart.

Young India, 6-9-'28

Whilst Gandhiji insists on a village worker living on a villager's diet not costing say more than three annas a day, he is far from insisting on starvation or mortification of the flesh. To a worker who had imposed on himself a strict regimen involving only one meal a day, consisting generally of 15 tolas of rice boiled, Amti (made of vegetables and Dal) and buttermilk, all costing only one anna per day, Gandhiji wrote :

" Your meal is very meagre, it is starvation diet. In my opinion, you are not making full use of the instrument that God has put at your disposal. Do you know the story of the talents that were taken away from him who did not know how to use them, or having known would not use them ?

" Mortification of the flesh is a necessity when the flesh rebels against one ; it is a sin when the flesh has come under subjection and can be used as an instrument of service. In other words, there is no inherent merit in mortification of the flesh."

Harijan, 2-11-'35

8

RENUNCIATION AND SELF-SACRIFICE

Renunciation does not mean abandoning the world and retiring into the forest. The spirit of renunciation should rule all the activities of life. A householder does not cease to be one, if he regards life as a duty rather than as an indulgence. A merchant, who operates in the sacrificial spirit, will have crores passing through his hands, but he will, if he follows the law, use his abilities for service. He will therefore not cheat or speculate, will lead a simple life, will not injure a living soul and will lose millions rather than harm anybody.

A life of sacrifice is the pinnacle of art, and is full of true joy. One who would serve will not waste a thought upon his own comforts, which he leaves to be attended to or neglected by his Master on High. He will not therefore encumber himself with everything that comes his way; he will take only what he strictly needs and leave the rest. He will be calm, free from anger and unruffled in mind even if he finds himself inconvenienced. His service, like virtue, is its own reward, and he will rest content with it.

Voluntary service of others demands the best of which one is capable, and must take precedence over service of self. In fact, the pure devotee consecrates himself to the service of humanity without any reservation whatever.

***From Yeravda Mandir*, 1945; pp. 57-60**

There should be no sorrow felt over one's sacrifice. That sacrifice which causes pain, loses its sacred character and will break down under stress. One gives up things that one considers to be injurious and therefore there should be pleasure attendant upon giving up.

***Young India*, 15-7-'26**

9

BREAD LABOUR

The law, that to live man must work, first came home to me upon reading Tolstoy's writing on Bread labour. But even before that I had begun to pay homage to it after reading Ruskin's *Unto This Last*. The divine law, that man must earn his bread by labouring with his own hands, was first stressed by a Russian writer named T. M. Bondaref. Tolstoy advertised it, and gave it wider publicity. In my view, the same principle has been set forth in the third chapter of the Gita, where we are told, that he who eats without offering sacrifice, eats stolen food. Sacrifice here can only mean Bread labour.

Reason too leads us to an identical conclusion. How can a man, who does not do body labour, have the right to eat? 'In the sweat of thy brow shalt thou eat thy bread,' says the Bible. A millionaire cannot carry on for long, and will soon get tired of his life, if he rolls in his bed all day long, and is even helped to his food. He, therefore, induces hunger by exercise, and helps himself to the food he eats. If every one, whether rich or poor, has thus to take exercise in some shape or form, why should it not assume the form of productive, i.e., Bread labour? No one asks the cultivator to take breathing exercise or to work his muscles. And more than nine tenths of humanity lives by tilling the soil. How much happier, healthier and more peaceful would the world become, if the remaining tenth followed the example of the overwhelming majority, at least to the extent of labouring enough for their food! And many hardships, connected with agriculture, would be easily redressed, if such people took a hand in it. Again invidious distinctions of rank would be abolished, when every one without exception acknowledged the obligation of Bread labour. It is common to all the Varnas. There is a world-wide conflict between capital and labour, and the poor envy the rich. If all worked for their bread, distinctions of rank would be obliterated ; the rich would still be there, but they would deem themselves only trustees of their property, and would use it mainly in the public interest.

Bread labour is a veritable blessing to one who would observe Non-violence, worship Truth and make the observance of Brahmacharya a natural act. This labour can truly be related to agriculture alone. But at present at any rate, everybody is not in a position to take to it. A person can therefore spin or weave, or take up carpentry or smithery, instead of tilling the soil, always regarding agriculture however to be the ideal. Every one must be his own scavenger. Evacuation is as necessary as eating ; and the best thing would be for every one to dispose of his own waste. If this is impossible, each family should see to its own scavenging. I have felt for years, that there must be something radically wrong, where scavenging has been made the concern of a separate class in society. We have no historical record of the man, who first assigned the lowest status to this essential sanitary service. Whoever he was, he by no means did us a good. We should, from our very childhood, have the idea impressed upon our minds that we are all scavengers, and the easiest way of doing so is, for every one who has realized this, to commence Bread labour as a scavenger. Scavenging, thus intelligently taken up, will help one to a true appreciation of the equality of man.

***From Yeravda Mandir*, 1945 ; pp. 35-37**

Sacrifices may be of many kinds. One of them may be Bread labour. If all laboured for their bread and no more, then there would be enough food and enough leisure for all. Then there would be no cry of over-population, no disease and no such misery as we see around. Such labour will be the highest form of sacrifice. Men will no doubt do many other things either through their bodies or through their minds, but all this will be labour of love for the common good. There will then be no rich and no poor, none high and none low, no touchable and no untouchable.

This may be an unattainable ideal. But we need not, therefore, cease to strive for it. Even if without fulfilling the whole law of sacrifice, that is, the law of our being, we performed physical labour enough for our daily bread, we should go a long way towards the ideal.

If we did so, our wants would be minimized, our food would be simple. We should then eat to live, not live to eat. Let anyone who doubts the accuracy of this proposition try to sweat for his bread, he will derive the greatest relish from the productions of his labour, improve his health and discover that many things he took were superfluities.

May not men earn their bread by intellectual labour? No. The needs of the body must be supplied by the body. 'Render unto Caesar that which is Caesar's' perhaps applies here well.

Mere mental, that is, intellectual labour is for the soul and is its own satisfaction. It should never demand payment. In the ideal State, doctors, lawyers and the like will work solely for the benefit of society, not for self. Obedience to law of Bread labour will bring about a silent revolution in the structure of society. Men's triumph will consist in substituting the struggle for existence by the struggle for mutual service. The law of the brute will be replaced by the law of man.

Return to the villages means a definite voluntary recognition of the duty of Bread labour and all it connotes. But says the critic, 'Millions of India's children are today living in the villages and yet they are living a life of semi-starvation.' This, alas! is but too true. Fortunately we know that theirs is not voluntary obedience. They would perhaps shirk body labour if they could, and even rush to the nearest city if they could be accommodated in it. Compulsory obedience to a master is a state of slavery, willing obedience to one's father is the glory of sonship. Similarly compulsory obedience to the law of Bread labour breeds poverty, disease and discontent. It is a state of slavery. Willing obedience to it must bring contentment and health. And it is health which is real wealth, not pieces of silver and gold. The Village Industries Association is an experiment in willing Bread labour.

Harijan, 29-6-'35

Q. Why should we insist on a Rabindranath or Raman earning his bread by manual labour? Is it not sheer wastage? Why should not brain workers be considered on a par with manual workers, for both of them perform useful social work?

A. Intellectual work is important and has an undoubted place in the scheme of life. But what I insist on is the necessity of physical labour. No man, I claim, ought to be free from that obligation. It will serve to improve even the quality of his intellectual output.

Harijan, 23-2-'47

10

SWADESHI

The votary of Swadeshi will, as a first duty, dedicate himself to the service of his immediate neighbours. This involves exclusion or even sacrifice of the interests of the rest, but the exclusion or the sacrifice would be only in appearance. Pure service of our neighbours can never, from its very nature, result in disservice to those who are far away, but rather the contrary. 'As with the individual, so with the universe' is an unfailing principle, which we would do well to lay to heart. On the other hand, a man who allows himself to be lured by 'the distant scene,' and runs to the ends of the earth for service, is not only foiled in his ambition, but also fails in his duty towards his neighbours. Take a concrete instance. In the particular place where I live, I have certain persons as my neighbours, some relations and dependents. Naturally, they all feel, as they have a right to, that they have a claim on me, and look to me for help and support. Suppose now I leave them all at once, and set out to serve people in a distant place. My decision would throw my little world of neighbours and dependents out of gear, while my gratuitous knight-errantry would, more likely than not, disturb the atmosphere in the new place. Thus a culpable neglect of my immediate neighbours, and an unintended disservice to the people whom I wish to serve, would be the first fruits of my violation of the principles of Swadeshi.

It is only when the doctrine of Swadeshi is wrongly understood, that mischief results. For instance, it would be a travesty of the doctrine of Swadeshi, if to coddle my family I set about grabbing money by all means fair or foul. The law of Swadeshi requires no more of me than to discharge my legitimate obligations towards my family by just means, and the attempt to do so will reveal to me the universal code of conduct. The practice of Swadeshi can never do harm to any one, and if it does, it is not Swadharma but egotism that moves me.

There may arise occasions, when a votary of Swadeshi may be called upon to sacrifice his family at the altar of universal service. Such an act of willing immolation will then constitute the highest service rendered to the family. 'Whosoever saveth his life shall lose it, and whosoever loseth his life for the Lord's sake shall find it,' holds good for the family group no less than for the individual. Take another instance. Supposing there is an outbreak of plague in my village, and in trying to serve the victims of the epidemic, I, my wife and children and all the rest of my family are wiped out of existence; then in inducing those dearest and nearest to join me, I will not have acted as the destroyer of my family, but on the contrary as its truest friend. In Swadeshi there is no room for selfishness; or if there is selfishness in it, it is of the highest type, which is not different from the highest altruism. Swadeshi in its purest form is the acme of universal service.

It was by following this line of argument, that I hit upon Khadi as the necessary and the most important corollary of the principle of Swadeshi in its application to society. 'What is the kind of service', I asked myself, 'what the teeming millions of India most need at the present time, that can be easily understood and appreciated by all, that is easy to perform and will at the same time enable the crores of our semi-starved countrymen to live ?' and the reply came, that it is the universalizing of Khadi or the spinning-wheel alone, that can fulfil these conditions.

Let no one suppose, that the practice of Swadeshi through Khadi would harm the foreign or Indian mill-owners. A thief, who is weaned from his vice, or is made to return the property that he has stolen, is not harmed thereby. On the contrary, he is the gainer, consciously in the one case, unconsciously in the other. Similarly, if all the opium-addicts or drunkards in the world were to shake themselves free from their vice, the canteen-keepers or the opium-vendors, who would be deprived of their custom, could not be said to be losers. They would be the gainers in the truest sense of the word. The elimination of the wages of sin is never a loss either to the individual concerned or to society ; it is pure gain.

It is the greatest delusion to suppose, that the duty of Swadeshi begins and ends with merely spinning some yarn anyhow and wearing Khadi made from it. Khadi is the first indispensable step towards the discharge of Swadeshi Dharma to society. But one often meets men, who wear Khadi, while in all other things they indulge their taste for foreign manufactures. Such men cannot be said to be practising Swadeshi. They are simply following the fashion. A votary of Swadeshi will carefully study his environment, and try to help his neighbours wherever possible, by giving preference to local manufactures, even if they are of an inferior grade or dearer in price than things manufactured elsewhere. He will try to remedy their defects, but will not, because of their defects, give them up in favour of foreign manufactures.

But even Swadeshi, like any other good things, can be ridden to death if it is made a fetish. That is a danger which must be guarded against. To reject foreign manufactures merely because they are foreign, and to go on wasting national time and money in the promotion in one's country of manufactures for which it is not suited would be criminal folly, and a negation of the Swadeshi spirit. A true votary of Swadeshi will never harbour illwill towards the foreigner, he will not be actuated by antagonism towards anybody on earth. Swadeshism is not a cult of hatred. It is a doctrine of selfless service, that has its roots in the purest Ahimsa, i.e. Love.

[This note on Swadeshi was not written in Yeravda Jail in 1930 but outside, after Gandhiji's release in 1931.]

From Yeravda Mandir, 1945; pp. 63-67

The broad definition of Swadeshi is the use of all home-made things to the exclusion of foreign things, in so far as such use is necessary for the protection of home-industry, more especially those industries without which India will become pauperized. In my opinion, therefore, Swadeshi which excludes the use of everything foreign no matter how beneficent it may be, and irrespective of the fact that it impoverishes nobody, is a narrow interpretation of Swadeshi.

Young India, 17-6-'26

11

RESPECT FOR ALL RELIGIONS

Religions are different roads converging to the same point. What does it matter that we take different roads, so long as we reach the same goal? In reality, there are as many religions as there are individuals.

Hind Swaraj, 1946; pp. 35-36

Ahimsa teaches us to entertain the same respect for the religious faiths of others as we accord to our own, thus admitting the imperfection of the latter. This admission will be readily made by a seeker of Truth, who follows the law of Love. If we had attained the full vision of Truth, we would no longer be mere seekers, but have become one with God, for Truth is God. But being only seekers, we prosecute our quest, and are conscious of our imperfection. And if we are imperfect ourselves, religion as conceived by us must also be imperfect. We have not realized religion in its perfection, even as we have not realized God. Religion of our conception, being thus imperfect, is always subject to a process of evolution and re-interpretation. Progress towards Truth, towards God, is possible only because of such evolution. And if all faiths outlined by men are imperfect, the question of comparative merit does not arise. All faiths constitute a revelation of Truth, but all are imperfect, and liable to error. Reverence for other faiths need not blind us to their faults. We must be keenly alive to the defects of our own faith also, yet not leave it on that account, but try to overcome those defects. Looking at all religions with an equal eye, we would not only not hesitate, but would think it our duty, to blend into our faith every acceptable feature of other faiths.

Even as a tree has a single trunk, but many branches and leaves, so there is one true and perfect Religion, but it becomes many, as it passes through the human medium. The one Religion is beyond all speech. Imperfect men put it into such language as they can command, and their words are interpreted by other men equally imperfect. Whose interpretation is to be held to be the right one? Everybody is right from his own standpoint, but it is not impossible that everybody is wrong. Hence the necessity of tolerance, which does not mean indifference to one's own faith, but a more intelligent and purer love for it. Tolerance gives us spiritual insight, which is as far from fanaticism as the north pole from the south. True knowledge of religion breaks down the barriers between faith and faith.

From Yeravda Mandir, 1945; pp. 38-40

There is one rule, however, which should always be kept in mind while studying all great religions, and that is that one should study them only through the writings of known votaries of the respective religions. For instance, if one wants to study the Bhagavata, one should do so not through a translation of it made by a hostile critic but one prepared by a lover of the Bhagavata. Similarly to study the Bible one should study it through the commentaries of devoted Christians. This study of other religions besides one's own will give one a grasp of the rock-bottom unity of all religions and afford a glimpse also of the universal and absolute truth which lies beyond the 'dust of creeds and faiths'.

Let no one even for a moment entertain the fear that a reverent study of other religions is likely to weaken or shake one's faith in one's own. The Hindu system of philosophy regards all religions as containing the elements of truth in them and enjoins an attitude of respect and reverence towards them all. This of course presupposes regard for one's own religion. Study and appreciation of other religions need not cause a weakening of that regard; it should mean extension of that regard to other religions.

Young India, 6-12-'28

I do not believe in people telling others of their faith, especially with a view to conversion. Faith does not admit of telling. It has to be lived and then it becomes self-propagating.

Young India, 20-10-'27

Religion is a very personal matter. We should by living the life according to our lights share the best with one another, thus adding to the sum total of human effort to reach God.

Harijan, 28-11-'36

12

ANTI-UNTOUCHABILITY

None can be born untouchable, as all are sparks of one and the same Fire. It is wrong to treat certain human beings as untouchables from birth.

This observance is not fulfilled merely by making friends with 'untouchables', but by loving all life as our own selves. Removal of untouchability means love for, and service of the whole world, and thus merges into Ahimsa. Removal of untouchability spells the breaking down of barriers between man and man, and between the various orders of Being. We find such barriers erected everywhere in the world.

From Yeravda Mandir, 1945; pp. 31, 33, 34

SECTION THREE: ECONOMIC ORDER

A. NON-VIOLENT ECONOMY

1

THE NON-VIOLENT BASIS

Under the new outlook we shall cease to think of getting what we can, but we shall decline to receive what all cannot get. It occurs to me that it ought not to be difficult to make a successful appeal to the masses in terms of economics and a fairly successful working of such an experiment must lead to immense and unconscious spiritual results. I do not believe that the spiritual law works on a field of its own. On the contrary, it expresses itself only through the ordinary activities of life. It thus affects the economic, the social and the political fields.

***Young India*, 3-9-'25**

2

HUMAN ELEMENT ESSENTIAL FOR ECONOMIC EFFICIENCY

Man is an engine whose motive power is the soul. The largest quantity of work will not be done by this curious engine for pay or under pressure. It will be done when the motive force, that is to say, the will or spirit of the creature, is brought to its greatest strength by its own proper fuel, namely by the affections. The universal law of the matter is that, assuming any given quantity of energy and sense in master and servant, the greatest material result obtainable by them will be not through antagonism to each other, but through affection for each other. Unselfish treatment will produce the most effective return. Treat the servant kindly with the idea of turning his gratitude to account, and you will get, as you deserve, no gratitude nor any value for your kindness ; but treat him kindly without any economical purpose, and all economical purposes will be answered ; here as elsewhere whoever will save his life shall lose it, whoso loses it shall find it.

Supposing an officer only desires to apply the rules of discipline so as, with least trouble to himself, to make the regiment most effective, he will not be able, by any rules, on this selfish principle, to develop the full strength of his subordinates. But if he has the most direct personal relations with his men, the most care for their interests, and the most value for their lives, he will develop their effective strength, through their affection for his own person and trust in his character, to a degree wholly unattainable by other means.

In his office as governor of the men employed by him, the merchant is invested with a paternal authority and responsibility. In most cases a youth entering a commercial establishment is withdrawn altogether from home influence ; his master must become his father ; else he has, for practical and constant help, no father at hand. So that the only means which the master has of doing justice to the men employed by him is to ask himself sternly whether he is dealing with such subordinates as he would with his own son, if compelled by circumstances to take such a position.

Supposing the captain of a frigate were obliged to place his own son in the position of a common sailor ; as he would then treat his son, he is bound always to treat every one of the men under him. So also supposing the master of a factory were obliged to place his own son in the position of an ordinary workman ; as he would then treat his son, he is bound always to treat every one of his men. This is the only effective, true or practical Rule which can be given on this point of economics.

And as the captain of a ship is bound to be the last man to leave his ship in case of wreck and to share his last crust with the sailors in case of famine, so the manufacturer, in any commercial crisis, is bound to take the suffering of it with his men, and even to take more of it for himself than he allows his men to feel; as a father would in a famine, shipwreck or battle, sacrifice himself for his son.

All this sounds very strange; the only real strangeness in the matter being, nevertheless, that it should so sound. For all this is true everlastingly and practically.

Gandhiji's Paraphrase of *Unto This Last*, 1951; pp. 8-11, 21-23

3

MEN ARE WEALTH, NOT GOLD AND SILVER

What is really desired, under the name of riches is, essentially, power over men; in its simplest sense, the power of obtaining for our own advantage the labour of servant, tradesman and artist. So that the art of becoming 'rich' in the common sense is not only the art of accumulating much money for ourselves but also of contriving that our neighbours shall have less. In accurate terms it is 'the art of establishing the maximum inequality in our own favour.'

Since the essence of wealth consists in power over men, will it not follow that the nobler and the more in number the persons are over whom it has power, the greater the wealth? Perhaps it may even appear after some consideration that the persons themselves *are* the wealth; not gold and silver. The true veins of wealth are purple — and not in Rock but in Flesh. The final consummation of all wealth is in producing as many as possible full-breathed, bright-eyed and happy-hearted human beings. In some far-away and yet undreamt-of hour I can even imagine that instead of adorning the turbans of her slaves with diamonds from Golkonda and thus showing off her material wealth, England, as a Christian mother, may at last attain to the virtues and the treasures of a non-Christian one and be able to lead forth her Sons, saying,

" These are MY Jewels."

Gandhiji's Paraphrase of *Unto This Last*, 1951; pp. 28, 29, 41, 42

Therefore there is no wealth but life. That country is the richest which nourishes the greatest number of noble and happy human beings; that man is richest who, having perfected the functions of his own life to the utmost, has also the widest helpful influence, both personal and by means of his possessions, over the lives of others.

Gandhiji's Paraphrase of *Unto This Last*, 1951; p. 57

4

A JUST WAGE

If I pay due wages to my man, I shall not be able to amass unnecessary riches, to waste money on luxuries and to add to the mass of poverty in the world. The workman who receives due wages from me will act justly to his subordinates. Thus the stream of justice will not dry up, but gather strength as it flows onward. And the nation with such a sense of justice will be happy and prosperous.

We thus find that the economists are wrong in thinking that competition is good for a nation. Competition only enables the purchaser to obtain his labour unjustly cheap, with the result that the rich grow richer and the poor poorer. In the long run it can only lead the nation to ruin. A workman should receive a just wage according to his ability. Even then there will be competition of a sort, but the people will be happy and skilful, because they will not have to underbid one another, but to acquire new skills in order to secure employment. This is the secret of the attractiveness of Government services in which salaries are fixed according to the gradation of posts. The candidate for it does not offer to work with a lower salary but only claims that he is abler than his competitors. The same is the case in the army and in the navy, where there is little corruption. But in trade and manufacture there is oppressive competition, which results in fraud, chicanery and theft. Rotten goods are manufactured. The manufacturer, the labourer, the consumer, — each is mindful of his own interest. This poisons all human intercourse. Labourers starve and go on strike. Manufacturers become rogues and consumers too neglect the ethical aspect of their own conduct. One injustice leads to many others, and in the end the employer, the operative and the customer are all unhappy and go to rack and ruin. The very wealth of the people acts among them as a curse.

True economics is the economics of justice. People will be happy in so far as they learn to do justice and be righteous. All else is not only vain but leads straight to destruction. To teach the people to get rich by hook or by crook is to do them an immense disservice.

Gandhiji's Paraphrase of *Unto This Last*, 1951; pp. 50-53

An economics that inculcates Mammon worship, and enables the strong to amass wealth at the expense of the weak, is a false and dismal science. It spells death. True economics, on the other hand, stands for social justice, it promotes the good of all equally including the weakest, and is indispensable for decent life.

Harijan, 9-10-'37

5

ECONOMIC EQUALITY

My idea of society is that while we are born equal, meaning that we have a right to equal opportunity, all have not the same capacity. It is, in the nature of things, impossible. For instance, all cannot have the same height, or colour or degree of intelligence, etc. ; therefore in the nature of things, some will have ability to earn more and others less. People with talents will have more, and they will utilize their talents for this purpose. If they utilize their talents kindly, they will be performing the work of the State. Such people exist as trustees, on no other terms. I would allow a man of intellect to earn more, I would not cramp his talent. But the bulk of his greater earnings must be used for the good of the State, just as the income of all earning sons of the father go to the common family fund.

Young India, 26-11-'31

The real implication of equal distribution is that each man shall have the wherewithal to supply all his natural wants and no more. For example, if one man has a weak digestion and requires only a quarter of a pound of flour for his bread and another needs a pound, both should be in a position to satisfy their wants. To bring this ideal into being the entire social order has got to be reconstructed. A society based on non-violence cannot nurture any other ideal. We may not perhaps be able to realize the goal, but we must bear it in mind and work unceasingly to near it. To the same extent as we progress towards our goal we shall find contentment and happiness, and to that extent too, shall we have contributed towards the bringing into being of a non-violent society.

Harijan, 25-8-'40

6

EQUALITY OF INCOME

Put your talents in the service of the country instead of converting them into £. s. d. If you are a medical man, there is disease enough in India to need all your medical skill. If you are a lawyer, there are differences and quarrels enough in India. Instead of fomenting more trouble patch up those quarrels and stop litigation. If you are an engineer, build model houses suited to the means and needs of our people and yet full of health and fresh air. There is nothing that you have learnt which cannot be turned to account. (The friend who asked the question was a Chartered Accountant and Gandhiji then said to him): There is a dire need everywhere for accountants to audit the accounts of Congress and its adjunct associations. Come to India — I will give you enough work and also your hire — 4 annas per day which is surely much more than millions in India get.

***Young India*, 5-11-'31**

Practice of law ought not to mean taking more daily than, say, a village carpenter's wage.

***Harijan*, 13-7-'40**

The Swaraj of my dream is the poor man's Swaraj. The necessaries of life should be enjoyed by you in common with those enjoyed by the princes and the moneyed men. But that does not mean that you should have palaces like theirs. They are not necessary for happiness. You or I would be lost in them. But, you ought to get all the ordinary amenities of life that a rich man enjoys. I have not the slightest doubt that Swaraj is not Purna Swaraj until these amenities are guaranteed to you under it.

From a Speech to the Labour Union of Ahmedabad.
***Young India*, 26-3-'31**

In answer to a question Gandhiji replied that if India was to live an exemplary life of independence which would be the envy of the world, all the Bhangis, doctors, lawyers, teachers, merchants and others would get the same wages for an honest day's work. Indian society may never reach the goal but it was the duty of every Indian to set his sail towards that goal and no other if India was to be a happy land.

Harijan, 16-3-'47

7

DECENTRALIZATION

I suggest that, if India is to evolve along non-violent lines, it will have to decentralize many things. Centralization cannot be sustained and defended without adequate force. Simple homes from which there is nothing to take away require no policing ; the palaces of the rich must have strong guards to protect them against dacoity. So must huge factories. Rurally organized India will run less risk of foreign invasion than urbanized India, well equipped with military, naval and air forces.

Harijan, 30-12-'39

You cannot build non-violence on a factory civilization, but it can be built on self-contained villages. Rural economy as I have conceived it, eschews exploitation altogether, and exploitation is the essence of violence. You have, therefore, to be rural-minded before you can be non-violent, and to be rural-minded you have to have faith in the spinning wheel.

Harijan, 4-11-'39

The end to be sought is human happiness combined with full mental and moral growth. I use the adjective moral as synonymous with spiritual. This end can be achieved under decentralization. Centralization as a system is inconsistent with non-violent structure of society.

Harijan, 18-1-'42

8

NON-VIOLENT OCCUPATIONS

Strictly speaking, no activity and no industry is possible without a certain amount of violence, no matter how little. Even the very process of living is impossible without a certain amount of violence. What we have to do is to minimize it to the greatest extent possible. Indeed the very word non-violence, a negative word, means that it is an effort to abandon the violence that is inevitable in life. Therefore whoever believes in Ahimsa will engage himself in occupations that involve the least possible violence. Thus, for instance, one cannot conceive of a man believing in non-violence carrying on the occupation of a butcher. Not that a meat-eater cannot be non-violent, but even a meat-eater believing in non-violence will not go in for Shikar, and he will not engage in war or war preparations. Thus there are many activities and occupations which necessarily involve violence and must be eschewed by a non-violent man. But there is agriculture without which life is impossible, and which does involve a certain amount of violence. The determining factor therefore is — is the occupation founded on violence? But since all activity involves some measure of violence, all we have to do is to minimize the violence involved in it. This is not possible without a heart-belief in non-violence. Suppose there is a man who does no actual violence, who labours for his bread, but who is always consumed with envy at other people's wealth or prosperity. He is not non-violent. A non-violent occupation is thus that occupation which is fundamentally free from violence and which involves no exploitation or envy of others.

Now I have no historical proof, but I believe that there was a time in India when village economics were organized on the basis of such non-violent occupations, not on the basis of the rights of man but on the duties of man. Those who engaged themselves in such occupations did earn their living, but their labour contributed to the good of the community. A carpenter, for instance, ministered to the needs of the village farmer. He got no cash payment but was paid in kind by the villagers. There could be injustice even in this system, but it would be reduced to a minimum. I speak from personal knowledge of the life in Kathiawad of over sixty years ago. There was more lustre in people's eyes, and more life in their limbs, than you find today. It was a life founded on unconscious Ahimsa.

Body labour was at the core of these occupations and industries, and there was no large-scale machinery. For when a man is content to own only so much land as he can till with his own labour, he cannot exploit others. Handicrafts exclude exploitation and slavery. Large-scale machinery concentrate wealth in the hands of one man who lords it over the rest who slave for him. For he may be trying to create ideal conditions for his workmen, but it is none the less exploitation which is a form of violence.

Harijan, 1-9-'40

9

TOWARDS SARVODAYA IN INDIA'S PAST

To observe morality is to attain mastery over our mind and our passions. We notice that the mind is a restless bird ; the more it gets the more it wants, and still remains unsatisfied. The more we indulge our passions the more unbridled they become. Our ancestors, therefore, set a limit to our indulgences. They saw that happiness was largely a mental condition. A man is not necessarily happy because he is rich, or unhappy because he is poor. The rich are often seen to be unhappy, the poor to be happy. Millions will always remain poor. Observing all this, our ancestors dissuaded us from luxuries and pleasures. We have managed with the same kind of plough as existed thousands of years ago. We have retained the same kind of cottages that we had in former times and our indigenous education remains the same as before. We have had no system of life-corroding competition. Each followed his own occupation or trade and charged a regulation wage. It was not that we did not know how to invent machinery, but our forefathers knew that, if we set our hearts after such things, we would become slaves and lose our moral fibre. They, therefore, after due deliberation, decided that we should only do what we could with our hands and feet. They saw that our real happiness and health consisted in a proper use of our hands and feet. They further reasoned that large cities were a snare and a useless encumbrance and that people would not be happy in them, that there would be gangs of thieves and robbers, prostitution and vice flourishing in them and that poor men would be robbed by rich men. They were, therefore, satisfied with small villages. They saw that kings and their swords were inferior to the sword of ethics, and they, therefore, held the sovereigns of the earth to be inferior to the Rishis and the Fakirs. A nation with a constitution like this is fitter to teach others than to learn from others. This nation had courts, lawyers and doctors, but they were all within bounds. Everybody knew that these professions were not particularly superior; moreover, these Vakils and Vaids did not rob people; they were considered people's dependents, not their masters. Justice was tolerably fair. The ordinary rule was to avoid courts. There were no touts to lure people into them. This evil, too, was noticeable only in and around capitals. The common people lived independently and followed their agricultural occupation. They enjoyed true Home Rule.

Hind Swaraj, 1908; ch. XIII

1

INDUSTRIALISM A CURSE

Industrialism is, I am afraid, going to be a curse for mankind. Industrialism depends entirely on your capacity to exploit, on foreign markets being open to you, and on the absence of competitors. It is because these factors are getting less and less every day for England, that its number of unemployed is mounting up daily. The Indian boycott was but a flea-bite. And if that is the state of England, a vast country like India cannot expect to benefit by industrialization. In fact, India, when it begins to exploit other nations — as it must do if it becomes industrialized — will be a curse for other nations, a menace to the world. And why should I think of industrializing India to exploit other nations? Don't you see the tragedy of the situation viz. that we can find work for our 300 millions unemployed, but England can find none for its three millions and is faced with a problem that baffles the greatest intellects of England? The future of industrialism is dark. England has got successful competitors in America, Japan, France, Germany. It has competitors in the handful of mills in India, and as there has been an awakening in India, even so there will be an awakening in South Africa with its vastly richer resources — natural, mineral and human. The mighty English look quite pigmies before the mighty races of Africa. They are noble savages after all, you will say. They are certainly noble, but no savages; and in the course of a few years the Western nations may cease to find in Africa a dumping ground for their wares. And if the future of industrialism is dark for the West, would it not be darker still for India?

***Young India*, 12-11-'31**

The present distress is undoubtedly insufferable. Pauperism must go. But industrialism is no remedy.

***Young India*, 7-10-'26**

2

MACHINERY

Machinery has its place; it has come to stay. But it must not be allowed to displace necessary human labour. An improved plough is a good thing. But if by some chance, one man could plough up by some mechanical invention of his the whole of the land of India, and control all the agricultural produce and if the millions had no other occupation, they would starve, and being idle, they would become dunces, as many have already become. There is hourly danger of many more being reduced to that unenviable state.

I would welcome every improvement in the cottage machine, but I know that it is criminal to displace hand-labour by the introduction of power-driven spindles unless one is at the same time ready to give millions of farmers some other occupation in their homes.

Young India, 5-11-'25

That use of machinery is lawful which subserves the interest of all.

Young India, 15-4-'26

I would favour the use of the most elaborate machinery if thereby India's pauperism and resulting idleness be avoided. I have suggested hand-spinning as the only ready means of driving away penury and making famine of work and wealth impossible. The spinning wheel itself is a piece of valuable machinery, and in my own humble way I have tried to secure improvements in it in keeping with the special conditions of India.

Young India, 3-11-'21

'Are you against all machinery?'

My answer is emphatically, 'No'. But, I am against its indiscriminate multiplication. I refuse to be dazzled by the seeming triumph of machinery. I am uncompromisingly against all destructive machinery. But simple tools and instruments and such machinery as saves individual labour and lightens the burden of the millions of cottages, I should welcome.

Young India, 17-6-'26

What I object to, is the *craze* for machinery, not machinery as such. The craze is for what they call labour-saving machinery. Men go on 'saving labour', till thousands are without work and thrown on the open streets to die of starvation. I want to save time and labour, not for a fraction of mankind, but for all; I want the concentration of wealth, not in the hands of a few, but in the hands of all. Today machinery merely helps a few to ride on the backs of millions. The impetus behind it all is not the philanthropy to save labour, but greed. It is against this constitution of things that I am fighting with all my might.

'Then you are fighting not against machinery as such, but against its abuses which are so much in evidence today.'

I would unhesitatingly say 'yes'; but I would add that scientific truths and discoveries should first of all cease to be mere instruments of greed. Then labourers will not be over-worked and machinery, instead of becoming a hindrance, will be a help. I am aiming, not at eradication of all machinery, but their limitation.

'When logically argued out, that would seem to imply that all complicated power-driven machinery should go.'

It might have to go but I must make one thing clear. The supreme consideration is man. The machine should not tend to make atrophied the limbs of man. For instance, I would make intelligent exceptions. Take the case of the Singer Sewing Machine. It is one of the few useful things ever invented, and there is a romance about the device itself. Singer saw his wife labouring over the tedious process of sewing and seaming with her own hands, and simply out of his love of her he devised the Sewing Machine in order to save her from unnecessary labour. He, however, saved not only her labour but also the labour of everyone who could purchase a Sewing Machine.

'But in that case there would have to be a factory for making these Singer Sewing Machines, and it would have to contain power-driven machinery of ordinary type.'

Yes, but I am socialist enough to say that such factories should be nationalized or State-controlled. They ought only to be working under the most attractive and ideal conditions, not for profit, but for the benefit of humanity, love taking the place of greed as the motive. It is an alteration in the conditions of labour that I want. This mad rush for wealth must cease, and the labourer must be assured, not only of a living wage, but a daily task that is not a mere drudgery. The machine will, under these conditions, be as much a help to the man working it as to the State, or the man who owns it. The present mad rush will cease, and the labourer will work (as I have said) under attractive and ideal conditions. This is but one of the exceptions I have in mind. The Sewing Machine had love at its back. The individual is the one supreme consideration. The saving of labour of the individual should be the object, and honest humanitarian considerations, and not greed, the motive. Replace greed by love and everything will come right.

Young India, 13-11-'24

'You are against this machine age, I see.'

To say that is to caricature my views. I am not against machinery as such, but I am totally opposed to it when it masters us.

'You would not industrialize India?'

I would indeed, in my sense of the term. The village communities should be revived. Indian villages produced and supplied to the Indian towns and cities all their wants. India became impoverished when our cities became foreign markets and began to drain the villages dry by dumping cheap and shoddy goods from foreign lands.

'You would then go back to the natural economy?'

Yes. But I am industrializing the village in a different way.

Harijan, 27-2-'37

The great mill industry may be claimed to be an Indian industry. But, in spite of its ability to compete with Japan and Lancashire, it is an industry that exploits the masses and deepens their poverty in exact proportion to its success over Khadi. In the modern craze for wholesale industrialization, my presentation has been questioned, if not brushed aside. It has been contended that the growing poverty of the masses, due to the progress of industrialization, is inevitable, and should therefore be suffered. I do not consider the evil to be inevitable, let alone to be suffered. The A. I. S. A. has successfully demonstrated the possibility of the villages manufacturing the whole of the cloth requirement of India, simply by employing the leisure hours of the nation in spinning and the anterior processes.

Harijan, 23-10-'37

I am personally opposed to great trusts and concentration of industries by means of elaborate machinery. If India takes to Khaddar and all it means, I do not lose the hope of India taking only as much of the modern machinery as may be considered necessary for the amenities of life and for labour-saving purposes.

Young India, 24-7-'24

The revival of the village is possible only when it is no more exploited. Industrialization on a mass scale will necessarily lead to passive or active exploitation of the villagers as the problems of competition and marketing come in. Therefore we have to concentrate on the village being self-contained, manufacturing mainly for use. Provided this character of the village industry is maintained, there would be no objection to villagers using even the modern machines and tools that they can make and can afford to use. Only they should not be used as a means of exploitation of others.

Harijan, 29-8-'36

I would categorically state my conviction that the mania for mass-production is responsible for the world-crisis. Granting for the moment that machinery may supply all the needs of humanity, still, it would concentrate production in particular areas, so that you would have to go about in a round about way to regulate distribution; whereas, if there is production and distribution both in the respective areas where things are required, it is automatically regulated, and there is less chance for fraud, none for speculation.

You see that these nations (Europe and America) are able to exploit the so-called weaker or unorganized races of the world. Once these races gain an elementary knowledge and decide that they are no more going to be exploited, they will simply be satisfied with what they can provide themselves. Mass-production, then, at least where the vital necessities are concerned, will disappear.

When production and consumption both become localized, the temptation to speed up production, indefinitely and at any price, disappears. All the endless difficulties and problems that our present-day economic system presents, too, would then come to an end.

There could be no unnatural accumulation of hoards in the pockets of the few, and want in the midst of plenty in regard to the rest.

'Then, you do not envisage mass-production as an ideal future of India?'

Oh yes, mass-production, certainly, but not based on force. After all, the message of the spinning wheel is that. It is mass-production, but mass-production in people's own homes. If you multiply individual production to millions of times, would it not give you mass-production on a tremendous scale? But I quite understand that your "mass-production" is a technical term for production by the fewest possible number through the aid of highly complicated machinery. I have said to myself that that is wrong. My machinery must be of the most elementary type which I can put in the homes of the millions.

'So, you are opposed to machinery, only because and when it concentrates production and distribution in the hands of the few?'

You are right, I hate privilege and monopoly. Whatever cannot be shared with the masses is taboo to me. That is all.

Harijan, 2-11-'34

C. CAPITAL AND LABOUR

1

CAPITAL AND LABOUR

We have come to believe that capital is all in all on earth. But a moment's thought would show that labour has at its disposal capital which the capitalist will never possess. Ruskin taught in his age that labour has unrivalled opportunities. But he spoke above our heads. At the present moment there is an Englishman, Sir Daniel Hamilton, who is really making the experiment. He is an economist. He is a capitalist also; but through his economic research and experiments he has come to the same conclusions as Ruskin has arrived at intuitively, and he has brought to labour a vital message. He says it is wrong to think that a piece of metal constitutes capital. He says it is wrong even to think that so much produce is capital; but he adds that if we go to the very source, it is labour that is capital, and that living capital is inexhaustible.

India's Case for Swaraj 1932; p. 393

I am for the establishment of right relations between capital and labour etc. I do not wish for the supremacy of the one over the other. I do not think there is any natural antagonism between them.

Young India, 8-1-'25

If capital is power, so is work. Either power can be used destructively or creatively. Either is dependent on the other. Immediately the worker realizes his strength, he is in a position to become a co-sharer with the capitalist instead of remaining his slave. If he aims at becoming the sole owner, he will most likely be killing the hen that lays the golden eggs.

Young India, 26-3-'31

2

NO MORAL RIGHT TO CAPITAL

Q. Whether a man accumulates material or moral wealth, he does so only through the help or co-operation of other members of society. Has he then the moral right to use any of it mainly for personal advantage ?

A. No, he has no moral right.

***Harijan*, 16-2-'47**

3

TRUSTEESHIP

Q. You have asked rich men to be trustees. Is it implied that they should give up private ownership in their property and create out of it a trust valid in the eyes of law and managed democratically ? How will the successor of the present incumbent be determined on his demise ?

A. In answer Gandhiji said that he adhered to the position taken by him years ago that everything belonged to God and was from God. Therefore it was for His people as a whole, not for a particular individual. When an individual had more than his proportionate portion he became a trustee of that portion for God's people.

God who was all-powerful had no need to store. He created from day to day, hence men also should in theory live from day to day and not stock things. If this truth was imbibed by the people generally, it would become legalized and trusteeship would become a legalized institution. He wished it became a gift from India to the world. Then there would be no exploitation and no reserves as in Australia and other countries for White men and their posterity. In these distinctions lay the seeds of a war more virulent than the last two. As to the successor, the trustee in office would have the right to nominate his successor subject to legal sanction.

***Harijan*, 23-2-'47**

My theory of 'trusteeship' is no make-shift, certainly no camouflage. I am confident that it will survive all other theories. It has the sanction of philosophy and religion behind it. That possessors of wealth have not acted up to the theory does not prove its falsity; it proves the weakness of the wealthy. No other theory is compatible with non-violence.

Harijan, 16-12-'39

Q. How would the successor of a trustee be determined? Will he only have the right of proposing a name, the right of finalization being vested in the State?

A. As he (Gandhiji) had said yesterday, choice should be given to the original owner who became the first trustee, but the choice must be finalized by the State. Such arrangement puts a check on the State as well as the individual.

Q. When the replacement of private by public property thus takes place through the operation of the theory of trusteeship, will the ownership vest in the State, which is an instrument of violence, or in associations of a voluntary character like village communes and municipalities, which may, of course, derive their final authority from State-made laws?

A. That question involved some confusion of thought. Legal ownership in the transformed condition was vested in the trustee, not in the State. It was in order to avoid confiscation that the doctrine of trusteeship came into play, retaining for society the ability of the original owner in his own right.

Nor did he, the speaker, hold that the State must always be based on violence. It might be so in theory, but the practice of the theory demanded a State which would for the most part be based on non-violence.

Harijan, 16-2-'47

4

GANDHIJI'S DOCTRINE OF TRUSTEESHIP

(*By Pyarelal*)

On our release from prison, we took up the question where we had left it in the Aga Khan Palace Detention Camp. Kishorlalbhai and Narharibhai joined in drawing up a simple, practical trusteeship formula. It was placed before Bapu who made a few changes in it. The final draft read as follows:

1. Trusteeship provides a means of transforming the present capitalist order of society into an egalitarian one. It gives no quarter to capitalism, but gives the present owning class a chance of reforming itself. It is based on the faith that human nature is never beyond redemption.

2. It does not recognize any right of private ownership of property except in as much as it may be permitted by society for its own welfare.

3. It does not exclude legislative regulation of the ownership and use of wealth.

4. Thus under State-regulated trusteeship, an individual will not be free to hold or use his wealth for selfish satisfaction or in disregard of the interest of society.

5. Just as it is proposed to fix a decent minimum living wage, even so a limit should be fixed for the maximum income that could be allowed to any person in society. The difference between such minimum and maximum incomes should be reasonable and equitable and variable from time to time so much so that the tendency would be towards obliteration of the difference.

6. Under the Gandhian economic order the character of production will be determined by social necessity and not by personal whim or greed.

Harijan, 25-10-'52

D. LANDLORD AND PEASANT

1

A MODEL ZAMINDAR

A model zamindar would at once reduce much of the burden the ryot is now bearing. He would come in intimate touch with the ryots and know their wants and inject hope into them in the place of despair which is killing the very life out of them. He will not be satisfied with the ryots' ignorance of the laws of sanitation and hygiene. He will reduce himself to poverty in order that the ryots may have the necessaries of life. He will study the economic condition of the ryots under his care, establish schools in which he will educate his own children side by side with those of the ryots. He will purify the village well and the village tank. He will teach the ryot to sweep his roads and clean his latrines by himself doing this necessary labour. He will throw open without reserve his own gardens for the unrestricted use of the ryot. He will use as hospital, school, or the like most of the unnecessary buildings which he keeps for his pleasure. If only the capitalist class will read the signs of the times, revise their notions of God-given right to all they possess, in an incredibly short space of time, the seven hundred thousand dung-heaps which today pass muster as villages can be turned into abodes of peace, health and comfort.

Young India, 5-12-'29

The zamindar is merey a tool of a system. It is not necessary to take up a movement against him. We have no quarrel with the zamindars as such, so long as they act well by the tenants.

Young India, 26-11-'31

2

TO ZAMINDARS

Let me assure you that I shall be no party to dispossessing propertied classes of their private property without just cause. My objective is to reach your heart and convert you so that you may hold all your private property in trust for your tenants and use it primarily for their welfare. I am quite clear that if strictly honest and unchallengeable referendum of our millions were to be taken, they would not vote for the wholesale expropriation of the propertied classes. I am working for the co-operation and co-ordination of capital and labour, of landlord and tenant.

But I must utter a note of warning. I have always told millowners that they are not exclusive owners of mills and workmen are equal sharers in ownership. In the same way, I would tell you that ownership of your land belongs as much to the ryots as to you, and you may not squander your gains in luxurious or extravagant living, but must use them for the wellbeing of ryots. Once you make your ryots experience a sense of kinship with you, and a sense of security that their interests as members of a family will never suffer at your hands, you may be sure that there cannot be a clash between you and them and no class war.

All your fears and misgivings, permit me to tell you, are those of guilty conscience. Wipe out injustices you may have been consciously or unconsciously guilty of. The ryots themselves have no greater ambition than to live in peace and freedom and they will never grudge your possession of property provided you use it for them.

Amrit Bazar Patrika, 2-8-'34

3

OWNERSHIP OF LAND

Real socialism has been handed down to us by our ancestors who taught: 'All land belongs to Gopal, where then is the boundary line? Man is the maker of that line and he can therefore unmake it.' Gopal literally means shepherd: it also means God. In modern language it means the State, i.e. the People. That the land today does not belong to the people is too true. But the fault is not in the teaching. It is in us who have not lived up to it.

I have no doubt that we can make as good an approach to it as is possible for any nation, not excluding Russia, and that without violence.

Harijan, 2-1-'37

4

PEASANTS AND LANDLORDS

The peasants must reject the doctrine that their holdings are absolutely theirs to the exclusion of the zamindars. They are or should be members of a joint family in which the zamindar is the head guarding their rights against encroachment. Whatever the law may be, the zamindari to be defensible must approach the conditions of a joint family.

Young India, 28-5-'31

5

CO-OPERATIVE FARMING

Gandhiji said in answer to a question that his notion of co-operation was that the land would be held in co-operation by the owners and tilled and cultivated also in co-operation. This would cause a saving of labour, capital, tools etc. The owners would work in co-operation and own capital, tools, animals, seeds etc. in co-operation. Co-operative farming of his conception would change the face of the land and banish poverty and idleness from their midst. All this was only possible if people became friends of one another and as one family.

Harijan, 9-3-'47

SECTION FOUR : SOCIAL ORDER

A. THE NARROWER SOCIETY — MAN

1

NON-VIOLENCE, A SOCIAL VIRTUE

I hold that non-violence is not merely a personal virtue. It is also a social virtue to be cultivated like the other virtues. Surely society is largely regulated by the expression of non-violence in its mutual dealings. What I ask for is an extension of it on a larger, national and international scale.

Harijan, 7-1-'39

2

THE INDIVIDUAL *v.* SOCIETY

I value individual freedom but you must not forget that man is essentially a social being. He has risen to his present status by learning to adjust his individualism to the requirements of social progress. Unrestricted individualism is the law of the beast of the jungle. We have to learn to strike the mean between individual freedom and social restraint. Willing submission to social restraint for the sake of the wellbeing of the whole society, enriches both the individual and the society of which one is a member.

Harijan, 27-5-'39

3

NO ROOM FOR UNTOUCHABILITY

If all that there is in the universe is pervaded by God, that is to say, if the Brahmana and the Bhangi, the learned man and the scavenger, the Ezhava and the Pariah, no matter what caste they belong to — if all these are pervaded by God, there is none that is high and none that is low, all are absolutely equal, equal because all are the creatures of that Creator.

Harijan, 30-1-'37

4

VARNASHRAMA

So far as I know anything at all of Hinduism, the meaning of Varna is incredibly simple. It simply means the following, on the part of us all, of the hereditary calling of our forefathers, in so far as that traditional calling is not inconsistent with fundamental ethics, and this only for the purpose of earning one's livelihood. You will realize that if all of us follow this law of Varna we would limit our material ambition, and our energy would be set free for exploring those vast fields whereby and wherethrough we can know God.

Young India, 20-10-'27

Varnashrama Dharma defines man's mission on this earth. He is not born day after day to explore avenues for amassing riches and to explore different means of livelihood; on the contrary man is born in order that he may utilize every atom of his energy for the purpose of knowing his Maker. It restricts him, therefore, for the purpose of holding body and soul together, to the occupation of his forefathers. That and nothing more or nothing less is Varnashrama Dharma.

Young India, 27-10-'27

5

CASTE AS VARNA

From the economic point of view, its value was once very great. It ensured hereditary skill; it limited competition. It was the best remedy against pauperism. And it had all the advantages of trade guilds. Although it did not foster adventure or invention there, it is not known to have come in the way either.

Historically speaking, caste may be regarded as man's experiment or social adjustment in the laboratory of Indian society. If we can prove it to be a success, it can be offered to the world as a leaven and as the best remedy against heartless competition and social disintegration born of avarice and greed.

Young India, 5-1-'21

I believe that every man is born in the world with certain natural tendencies. Every person is born with certain definite limitations which he cannot overcome. From a careful observation of those limitations the law of Varna was deduced. It establishes certain spheres of action for certain people with certain tendencies. This avoided all unworthy competition. Whilst recognizing limitations the law of Varna admitted of no distinctions of high and low; on the one hand it guaranteed to each the fruits of his labours, and on the other it prevented him from pressing upon his neighbour. This great law has been degraded and fallen into disrepute. But my conviction is that an ideal social order will only be evolved when the implications of this law are fully understood and given effect to.

The Modern Review, Oct. 1935; p. 413

6

INTERMARRIAGE

In Varnashrama there was and there should be no prohibition of intermarriage or interdining.

Though there is in Varnashrama no prohibition against intermarriage and interdining, there can be no compulsion. It must be left to the unfettered choice of the individual as to where he or she will marry or dine. If the law of Varnashrama was observed there would naturally be a tendency, so far as marriage is concerned, for people to restrict the marital relations to their own Varna.

Harijan, 16-11-'35

There should be a breach in the double wall of caste and province. If India is one and indivisible, surely there should be no artificial divisions creating innumerable little groups which would neither interdine nor intermarry.

Harijan, 25-7-'36

Q. You advocate inter-caste marriages. Do you also favour marriage between Indians professing different religions?

A. Though Gandhiji admitted that he had not always held the view, he had come to the conclusion long ago that an inter-religious marriage was a welcome event whenever it took place. His stipulation was that such connection was not a product of lust. In his opinion the latter was no marriage. It was illicit intercourse. Marriage in his estimation was a sacred institution. Hence there must be mutual friendship, either party having equal respect for the religion of the other. There was no question in this of conversion. Hence the marriage ceremony would be performed by the priests belonging to either faith. This happy event could take place when the communities shed mutual enmity and had regard for the religions of the world.

Harijan, 16-3-'47

7

THE PLACE OF WOMEN

The two (man and woman) live the same life, have the same feelings. Each is a complement of the other. The one cannot live without the other's active help.

But somehow or other man has dominated woman from ages past, and so woman has developed an inferiority complex. She has believed in the truth of man's interested teaching that she is inferior to him. But the seers among men have recognized her equal status.

Nevertheless there is no doubt that at some point there is bifurcation. Whilst both are fundamentally one, it is also equally true that in the form there is a vital difference between the two. Hence the vocations of the two must also be different. The duty of motherhood, which the vast majority of women will always undertake, requires qualities which man need not possess. She is passive, he is active. She is essentially mistress of the house. He is the bread-winner. She is the keeper and distributor of the bread. She is the care-taker in every sense of the term. The art of bringing up the infants of the race is her special and sole prerogative. Without her care the race must become extinct.

In my opinion it is degrading both for man and woman that woman should be called upon or induced to forsake the hearth and shoulder the rifle for the protection of that hearth. It is a reversion to barbarity and the beginning of the end. In trying to ride the horse that man rides, she brings herself and him down. The sin will be on man's head for tempting or compelling his companion to desert her special calling. There is as much bravery in keeping one's home in good order and condition as there is in defending it against attack from without.

As I have watched millions of peasants in their natural surroundings and as I watch them daily in little Segaon, the natural division of spheres of work has forced itself on my attention. There are no women black-smiths and carpenters. But men and women work on the fields, the heaviest work being done by the males. The women keep and manage the homes. They supplement the meagre resources of the family, but man remains the main bread-winner.

The division of the spheres of work being recognized, the general qualities and culture required are practically the same for both the sexes.

My contribution to the great problem lies in my presenting for acceptance Truth and Ahimsa in every walk of life, whether for individuals or nations. I have hugged the hope that in this woman will be the unquestioned leader and, having thus found her place in human evolution, she will shed her inferiority complex.

I have suggested in these columns that woman is the incarnation of Ahimsa. Ahimsa means infinite love, which again means infinite capacity for suffering. Who but woman, the mother of man, shows this capacity in the largest measure ? She shows it as she carries the infant and feeds it during nine months and derives joy in the suffering involved. What can beat the suffering caused by the pangs of labour ? But she forgets them in the joy of creation. Who again suffers daily so that her babe may wax from day to day ? Let her transfer that love to the whole of humanity, let her forget that she ever was or can be the object of man's lust. And she will occupy her proud position by the side of man as his mother, maker and silent leader. It is given to her to teach the art of peace to the warring world thirsting for that nectar. She can become the leader in Satyagraha which does not require the learning that books give but does require the stout heart that comes from suffering and faith.

My good nurse in the Sassoon Hospital, Poona, as I was lying on a sick-bed years ago, told me the story of a woman who refused to take chloroform because she would not risk the life of the babe she was carrying. She had to undergo a painful operation. The only anaesthetic she had was her love for the babe, to save whom no suffering was too great. Let not women, who can count many such heroines among them, ever despise their sex or deplore that they were not born men. The contemplation of that heroine often makes me envy woman the status that is hers, if she only knew. There is as much reason for man to wish that he was born a woman as for woman to do otherwise. But the wish is fruitless. Let us be happy in the state to which we are born and do the duty for which nature has destined us.

Harijan, 24-2-'40

8

EQUAL RIGHTS FOR THE SEXES

As a general rule, Gandhiji said, he was for one man one wife for life, and one woman one husband for life. Custom had familiarized women in the so-called higher castes with enforced widowhood. Contrary was the rule with men. He called it a disgrace, but whilst society was in that pitiable condition, he advocated widow remarriage for all young widows. He believed in equality of the sexes and, therefore, he could only think of the same rights for women as men.

Harijan, 16-3-'47

9

MARRIAGE

The wife is not the husband's bondslave, but his companion and his helpmate, and an equal partner in all his joys and sorrows — as free as the husband to choose her own path.

Autobiography, 1948 ; p. 38

I detest child marriages. I shudder to see a child widow, and shiver with rage when a husband just widowed contracts with brutal indifference another marriage. I deplore the criminal indifference of parents who keep their daughters utterly ignorant and illiterate and bring them up only for the purpose of marrying them off to some young man of means.

Young India, 21-7-'21

What is Kanyadan in the case of little children ? Has a father any rights of property over his children ? He is their protector not owner. And he forfeits the privilege of protecting when he abuses it by seeking to barter away the liberty of the ward.

The least that a parent, who has so abused his trust as to give in marriage an infant to an old man in his dotage or to a boy hardly in his teens, can do, is to purge himself of his sin by remarrying his daughter when she becomes widowed. As I have said in a previous note, such marriages should be declared null and void from the beginning.

Young India, 11-11-'26

Marriage is a natural thing in life, and to consider it derogatory in any sense is wholly wrong. The ideal is to look upon marriage as a sacrament and therefore to lead a life of self-restraint in the married estate.

Harijan, 22-3-'42

10

WIDOWHOOD

Voluntary widowhood consciously adopted by a woman who has felt the affection of a partner adds grace and dignity to life, sanctifies the home and uplifts religion itself. Widowhood imposed by religion or custom is an unbearable yoke and defiles the home by secret vice and degrades religion.

If we would be pure, if we would save Hinduism, we must rid ourselves of this poison of enforced widowhood. The reform must begin by those who have girl widows taking courage in both their hands and seeing that the child widows in their charge are duly and well married — not remarried. They were never really married.

***Young India*, 5-8-'26**

11

DIVORCE

Marriage confirms the right of union between two partners to the exclusion of all the others when in their joint opinion they consider such union to be desirable, but it confers no right upon one partner to demand obedience of the other to one's wish for union. What should be done when one partner on moral or other grounds cannot conform to the wishes of the other is a separate question. Personally, if divorce was the only alternative, I should not hesitate to accept it, rather than interrupt my moral progress, — assuming that I want to restrain myself on purely moral grounds.

***Young India*, 8-10-'25**

12

CONTRACEPTION

If it is contended that birth control is necessary for the nation because of over-population, I dispute the proposition. It has never been proved. In my opinion, by a proper land-system, better agriculture and a supplementary industry, this country is capable of supporting twice as many people as there are today.

Young India, 2-4-'25

Q. For the sake of the mother whose health is drained away by too many children and for the sake of the children themselves, may not birth control through contraceptives be resorted to as the next best thing to self-control?

A. Women should have to resist their husbands. If contraceptives are resorted to, frightful results will follow. Men and women will be living for sex alone. They will become soft-brained, unhinged, in fact mental and moral wrecks.

Q. Even in exceptional cases where women are too weak for childbearing or where either of the parents is diseased can't this method be resorted to?

A. No. In the cases stated above it is better that husband and wife should live apart.

I consider it inhuman to impose sterilization law on the people. But in cases of individuals with chronic diseases, it is desirable to have them sterilized if they are agreeable to it. Sterilization is a sort of contraceptive and though I am against the use of contraceptives in case of women, I do not mind voluntary sterilization in case of man since he is the aggressor.

Amrit Bazar Patrika, 12-1-'35

I have felt that during the years still left to me if I can drive home to women's minds the truth that they are free, we shall have no birth control problem in India. If they will only learn to say 'no' to their husbands when they approach them carnally....The real problem is that they do not want to resist them. It boils down to education. I want woman to learn the primary right of resistance. She thinks now that she has not got it. Among the women of India it is most difficult to drive home this truth. If I were to devote myself to birth control I would miss this primary education.

If you eliminate birth control there would be other methods. As soon as you agree to eliminate certain methods as harmful, you are bound to find others.

From a Report by Mrs. Margaret Sanger in *Asia*, Nov. '35.

B. THE LARGER SOCIETY—ANIMALS

1

COW PROTECTION

Cow protection to me is one of the most wonderful phenomena in human evolution. It takes the human being beyond his species. The cow to me means the entire sub-human world. Man through the cow is enjoined to realize his identity with all that lives. Why the cow was selected for apotheosis is obvious to me. The cow was in India the best companion. She was the giver of plenty. Not only did she give milk, but she also made agriculture possible. The cow is a poem of pity. One reads pity in the gentle animal. She is the mother to millions of Indian mankind. Protection of the cow means protection of the whole dumb creation of God. The ancient seer, whoever he was, began with the cow. The appeal of the lower orders of creation is all the more forcible because it is speechless.

Young India, 6-10-'21

A Hindu who protects the cow should protect every animal. But taking all things into consideration, we may not cavil at his protecting the cow because he fails to protect the other animals. The only question therefore to consider is whether he is right in protecting the cow. And he cannot be wrong in so doing if non-killing of animals generally may be regarded as a duty for one who believes in Ahimsa. And every Hindu, and for that matter every man of religion, does so. The duty of non-killing animals generally and therefore protecting them must be accepted as an indisputable fact. It is then so much to the credit of Hinduism that it has taken up cow protection as a duty. And he is a poor specimen of Hinduism who stops merely at cow protection when he can extend the arm of protection to other animals. The cow merely stands as a symbol, and protection of the cow is the least he is expected to undertake.

Young India, 11-11-'26

In its finer or spiritual sense the term cow protection means the protection of every living creature. Our Rishis made the startling discovery (and every day I feel more and more convinced of its truth) that sacred texts and inspired writings yield their truth only in proportion as one has advanced in the practice of Ahimsa and Truth. The greater the realization of Truth and Ahimsa the greater the illumination. These same Rishis declared that cow protection was the supreme duty of a Hindu and that its performance brought one Moksha i.e. salvation. Now I am not ready to believe that by merely protecting the animal cow, one can attain Moksha. For Moksha, one must completely get rid of one's lower feelings like attachment, hatred, anger, jealousy etc. It follows, therefore, that the meaning of cow protection in terms of Moksha must be much wider and far more comprehensive than is commonly supposed. The cow protection which can bring one Moksha must from its very nature include the protection of everything that feels. Therefore in my opinion, every little breach of the Ahimsa principle, like causing hurt by harsh speech to any one, man, woman or child, to cause pain to the weakest and the most insignificant creature on earth would be a breach of the principle of cow protection, would be tantamount to the sin of beef-eating — different from it in degree, if at all, rather than in kind.

Young India, 29-1-'25

2

NON-KILLING OF ANIMALS

To cause pain or wish ill to or to take the life of any living being out of anger or a selfish intent is Himsa. On the other hand, after a calm and clear judgment to kill or cause pain to a living being with a view to its spiritual or physical benefit from a pure, selfless intent may be the purest form of Ahimsa. Each such case must be judged individually and on its own merits. The final test as to its violence or non-violence is after all the intent underlying the act.

Young India, 4-10-'28

My Ahimsa is my own. I am not able to accept in its entirety the doctrine of non-killing of animals. I have no feeling in me to save the life of those animals who devour or cause hurt to man. I consider it wrong to help in the increase of their progeny. Therefore, I will not feed ants, monkeys, or dogs. I will never sacrifice a man's life in order to save theirs.

Thinking along these lines I have come to the conclusion that to do away with monkeys where they have become a menace to the wellbeing of man is pardonable. Such killing becomes a duty. The question may arise as to why this rule should not also apply to human beings. It cannot because, however bad, they are as we are. Unlike the animal, God has given man the faculty of reason.

Harijan, 5-5-'46

3

UNIVERSAL BROTHERHOOD

In the purest type of Hinduism a Brahmana, an ant, an elephant and a dog-eater (Shwapaka) are of the same status. Hinduism insists on the brotherhood not only of all mankind but of all that lives. It is a conception which makes one giddy, but we have to work up to it. The moment we have restored real living equality between man and man, we shall be able to establish equality between man and the whole creation. When that day comes we shall have peace on earth and goodwill among men.

Harijan, 28-3-'36

4

ANIMAL SACRIFICE

It does not matter, that animal sacrifice is alleged to find a place in the Vedas. It is enough for us that such sacrifice cannot stand the fundamental tests of Truth and Non-violence. I readily admit my incompetence in Vedic scholarship. But the incompetence, so far as this subject is concerned, does not worry me, because even if the practice of animal sacrifice be proved to have been a feature of Vedic society, it can form no precedent for a votary of Ahimsa.

From Yeravda Mandir, 1945; pp. 53, 54

SECTION FIVE: POLITICAL ORDER

A. SARVODAYA STATE

1

CHARACTER TO BE THE BASIS

Swaraj really means self-control. Only he is capable of self-control who observes the rules of morality, does not cheat or give up truth, and does his duty to his parents, wife and children, servants and neighbours. Such a man is in enjoyment of Swaraj, no matter where he lives. A State enjoys Swaraj if it can boast of a large number of such good citizens.

Swaraj * cannot be attained by the erection of huge factories. Gold and silver may be accumulated but they will not lead to the establishment of Swaraj. Ruskin has proved this to the hilt. Western civilization is a mere baby, a hundred or only fifty years old. And yet it has reduced Europe to a sorry plight. Let us pray that India is saved from the fate that has overtaken Europe, where the nations are poised for an attack on one another, and are silent only because of the stockpiling of armaments. Some day there will be an explosion, and then Europe will be a veritable hell on earth. Non-White races are looked upon as legitimate prey by every European State. What else can we expect where covetousness is the ruling passion in the breasts of men? Europeans pounce upon new territories like crows upon a piece of meat. I am inclined to think that this is due to their mass-production factories.

India must indeed have Swaraj but she must have it by righteous methods. Our Swaraj must be real Swaraj, which cannot be attained by either violence or industrialization. India was once a golden land, because Indians

* True democracy or rule of the people, i.e. Sarvodaya. — Ed.

then had a heart of gold. The land is still the same but is a desert because we are corrupt. It can become a land of gold again only if the base metal of our present national character is transmuted into gold. The philosopher's stone which can effect this transformation is a little word of two syllables — Satya (Truth). If every Indian sticks to Truth, Swaraj will come to us of its own accord.

(Gandhiji's Conclusion to his Paraphrase of *Unto This Last*, pp. 61-64)

True democracy or the Swaraj of the masses can never come through untruthful and violent means, for the simple reason that the natural corollary to their use would be to remove all opposition through the suppression or extermination of the antagonists. That does not make for individual freedom. Individual freedom can have the fullest play only under a regime of unadulterated Ahimsa.

Harijan, 27-5-'39

2

SARVODAYA DEMOCRACY

In this structure composed of innumerable villages, there will be ever widening, never ascending circles. Life will not be a pyramid with the apex sustained by the bottom. But it will be an oceanic circle whose centre will be the individual always ready to perish for the village, the latter ready to perish for the circle of villages, till at last the whole becomes one life composed of individuals, never aggressive in their arrogance but ever humble, sharing the majesty of the oceanic circle of which they are integral units.

Therefore, the outermost circumference will not wield power to crush the inner circle but will give strength to all within and derive its own strength from it. I may be taunted with the retort that this is all Utopian and, therefore, not worth a single thought. If Euclid's point, though incapable of being drawn by human agency, has an imperishable value, my picture has its own for mankind to live. Let India live for this true picture, though never realizable in its completeness. We must have a proper picture of what we want, before we can have something approaching it. If there ever is to be a republic of every village in India, then I claim verity for my picture in which the last is equal to the first or, in other words, no one is to be the first and none the last.

Harijan, 28-7-'46

True democracy cannot be worked by twenty men sitting at the centre. It has to be worked from below by the people of every village.

Harijan, 18-1-'48

If we want Swaraj to be built on non-violence, we will have to give the villages their proper place.

Harijan, 20-1-'40

3

THE GOAL

Under Swaraj based on non-violence nobody is anybody's enemy, everybody contributes his or her due quota to the common goal, all can read and write, and their knowledge keeps growing from day to day. Sickness and disease are reduced to the minimum. No one is a pauper and labour can always find employment. There is no place under such a government for gambling, drinking and immorality or for class hatred. The rich will use their riches wisely and usefully, and not squander them in increasing their pomp and worldly pleasures. It should not happen that a handful of rich people should live in jewelled palaces and the millions in miserable hovels devoid of sunlight or ventilation. Hindu-Muslim differences, untouchability, vertical differences between high and low, these must not be.

[From an appeal issued to the people of Rajkot by Gandhiji]

Harijan, 25-3-'39

4

AN INDIAN GOVERNOR

1. An Indian Governor should, in his own person and in his surroundings, be a teetotaller. Without this, prohibition of the fiery liquid is wellnigh inconceivable.

2. He and his surroundings should represent hand-spinning as a visible token of identification with the dumb millions of India, a token of the necessity of 'bread labour' and organized non-violence as against organized violence on which the society of today seems to be based.

3. He must dwell in a cottage accessible to all, though easily shielded from gaze, if he is to do efficient work. The British Governor naturally represented British might. For him and his was erected a fortified residence — a palace to be occupied by him and his numerous vassals who sustained his empire. The Indian prototype may keep somewhat pretentious buildings for receiving princes and ambassadors of the world. For these, being guests of the Governor should constitute an education in what "Even Unto This Last" — equality of all — should mean in concrete terms. For him no expensive furniture, foreign or indigenous. Plain living and high thinking must be his motto, not to adorn his entrance but to be exemplified in daily life.

4. For him there can be no untouchability in any form whatsoever, no caste or creed or colour distinction. He must represent the best of all religions and all things Eastern or Western. Being a citizen of India, he must be a citizen of the world. Thus simply, one reads, did the Khalif Omar, with millions of treasure at his feet, live; thus lived Janaka of ancient times; thus lived, as I saw him, the Master of Eton in his residence in the midst of, and surrounded by, the sons of the Lords and Nabobs of the British Isles. Will the Governors of India of the famished millions do less?

5. He will speak the language of the province of which he is the Governor and Hindustani, the lingua franca of India written in the Nagari or Urdu script. This is neither Sanskritized Hindi nor Persianized Urdu. Hindustani is emphatically the language which is spoken by the millions north of the Vindhya Range.

This does not pretend to be an exhaustive list of the virtues that an Indian Governor should represent. It is merely illustrative.

Harijan, 24-8-'47

5

POLITICAL POWER

To me political power is not an end but one of the means of enabling people to better their condition in every department of life. Political power means capacity to regulate national life through national representatives. If national life becomes so perfect as to become self-regulated, no representation becomes necessary. There is then a state of enlightened anarchy. In such a state everyone is his own ruler. He rules himself in such a manner that he is never a hindrance to his neighbour. In the ideal state, therefore, there is no political power because there is no State. But the ideal is never fully realized in life. Hence the classical statement of Thoreau that that government is best which governs the least.

Young India, 2-7-'31

I look upon an increase in the power of the State with the greatest fear, because, although while apparently doing good by minimizing exploitation, it does the greatest harm to mankind by destroying individuality which lies at the root of all progress.

The State represents violence in a concentrated and organized form. The individual has a soul, but as the State is a soulless machine, it can never be weaned from violence to which it owes its very existence.

It is my firm conviction that if the State suppressed capitalism by violence, it will be caught in the coils of violence itself and fail to develop non-violence at any time.

What I would personally prefer, would be, not a centralization of power in the hands of the State but an extention of the sense of trusteeship ; as in my opinion, the violence of private ownership is less injurious than the violence of the State. However, if it is unavoidable, I would support a minimum of State-ownership.

What I disapprove of is an organization based on force which a State is. Voluntary organization there must be.

The Modern Review, 1935, p. 412

In the democracy which I have envisaged, a democracy established by non-violence, there will be equal freedom for all. Everybody will be his own master.

Gandhiji's Correspondence with the Government, 1942-44, p. 173

6

SELF-GOVERNMENT

As every country is fit to eat, to drink and to breathe, even so is every nation fit to manage its own affairs, no matter how badly.

Young India, 15-10-'31

Self-government means continuous effort to be independent of government control whether it is foreign government or whether it is national. Swaraj government will be a sorry affair if people look up to it for the regulation of every detail of life.

Young India, 6-8-'25

By Swaraj I mean the government of India by the consent of the people as ascertained by the largest number of the adult population, male or female, native born or domiciled, who have contributed by manual labour to the service of the State and who have taken the trouble of having their names registered as voters. I hope to demonstrate that real Swaraj will come not by the acquisition of authority by a few but by the acquisition of the capacity by all to resist authority when abused. In other words,

Swaraj is to be attained by educating the masses to a sense of their capacity to regulate and control authority.

Young India, 29-1-'25

By political independence I do not mean an imitation of the British House of Commons or the Soviet rule of Russia or the Fascist rule of Italy or the Nazi rule of Germany. They have systems suited to their genius. We must have ours suited to ours. What that can be is more than I can tell. I have described it as Ramaraj, i.e. sovereignty of the people based on pure moral authority.

Harijan, 2-1-'37

7

THE RIGHT OF MINORITIES

The rule of majority has a narrow application, i.e. one should yield to the majority in matters of detail. But it is slavery to be amenable to the majority, no matter what its decisions are. Democracy is not a state in which people act like sheep. Under democracy individual liberty of opinion and action is jealously guarded. I therefore believe that the minority has a perfect right to act differently from the majority as long as it does not act in the name of the Congress.

Young India, 2-3-'22

In matters of conscience the law of majority has no place.

Young India, 4-8-'20

8

FRANCHISE

Gandhiji swore by the franchise of all adults, male and female, above the age of twentyone or even eighteen. He would bar old men like himself. They were of no use as voters. India and the rest of the world did not belong to those who were on the point of dying. To them belonged death, life to the young. Thus he would have a bar against persons beyond a certain age, say fifty, as he would against youngsters below eighteen.

Side by side with adult franchise, or even before that, he pleaded for universal education, not necessarily literary except as perhaps an aid. He would give them all sufficient knowledge in the rich languages of which any country would be proud. Education in the understanding of the rights of citizenship was a short-term affair if they were honest and earnest.

Harijan, 2-3-'47

9

PROVINCIALISM

Gandhiji held that the people of all the provinces belonged to India and India belonged to all. The only condition was that no one could go and settle in another province to exploit it or rule it or to injure its interest in any way. All were servants of India and they lived only in the spirit of service.

Harijan, 7-9-'47

A non-Bihari who settles in Bihar must do so to serve Bihar, not to exploit it.

What about the services? It seems that if the provinces are all to make equal progress in all directions, the services should be largely confined to the inhabitants of the province concerned for the sake of India as a whole.

In regard to people from outside settling in a province, Gandhiji observed: Naturally, they should not form a separate colony as if they were foreigners. 'Live in Rome as the Romans do', is a sound commonsense maxim so long as it does not apply to Roman vices. The process of progressive blending must be one of rejecting the bad and absorbing the good. As a Gujarati in Bengal, I must quickly absorb all that is good in Bengal and never touch that which is bad; I must ever serve Bengal, never selfishly exploit it. The bane of our life is our exclusive provincialism, whereas my province must be co-extensive with the Indian boundary so that ultimately it extends to the boundary of the earth. Else it perishes.

Harijan, 21-9-'47

10

THE STATE TO BE SECULAR

The State should undoubtedly be secular. Everyone living in it should be entitled to profess his religion without let or hindrance, so long as the citizen obeyed the common law of the land.

Harijan, 24-8-'47

B. ITS EXTERNAL RELATIONS

1

PARTNERSHIP WITH BRITAIN

I should love to be an equal partner with Britain sharing her joys and sorrows. But it must be a partnership on equal terms.

Q. Do you think that India would unite her fortunes inextricably with Britain?

A. Yes, so long as she remains a partner. But if she discovers that the partnership is like one between a giant and a dwarf or if it is utilized for the exploitation of the other races of the earth, she would dissolve it. The aim is the common good of all nations of the earth and if it cannot be achieved I have patience enough to wait for ages rather than patch up an unnatural partnership.

Young India, 12-11-'31

The partnership must mean that exploitation shall cease, and if Great Britain should not desist from it, India should sever the connection.

What about the South African possessions? I would not insist on a transformation of Britain's relations with them, as a condition precedent to our partnership. But I should certainly strive to work for the deliverance of those South African races which, I can say from experience, are ground down under exploitation. Our deliverance must mean their deliverance. But, if that cannot come about, I should have no interest in a partnership with Britain, even if it were of benefit to India. Speaking for myself, I would say that the partnership, giving the promise of a world set free from exploitation, would be a proud privilege for my nation and I would maintain it for ever. But India cannot reconcile herself in any shape or form to any policy of exploitation.

Young India, 19-11-'31

2

RELATION TO OTHER NATIONS

My patriotism is not exclusive; it is calculated not only not to hurt another nation but to benefit all in the true sense of the word. India's freedom as conceived by me can never be a menace to the world.

Young India, 3-4-'24

I would like to see India free and strong so that she may offer herself as a willing and pure sacrifice for the betterment of the world. The individual, being pure, sacrifices himself for the family, the latter for the village, the village for the district, the district for the province, the province for the nation, the nation for all.

Young India, 17-9-'25

My notion of Purna Swaraj is not isolated independence but healthy and dignified interdependence.

Young India, 26-3-'31

Through Swaraj we would serve the whole world.

Young India, 16-4-'31

There is no limit to extending our services to our neighbours across State-made frontiers. God never made those frontiers.

Young India, 31-12-'31

3

INTERNATIONAL ORGANIZATION FOR PEACE

There will be an international league only when all the nations, big or small, composing it are fully independent. The nature of that independence will correspond to the extent of non-violence assimilated by the nations concerned. One thing is certain. In a society based on non-violence, the smallest nation will feel as tall as the tallest. The idea of superiority and inferiority will be wholly obliterated.

Harijan, 11-2-'39

Q. Do you foresee the possibility of the world being united under one central governing body composed of representatives of the component parts ?

A. That is the only condition on which the world can live.

Harijan, 8-6-'47

SECTION SIX: RESISTANCE TO EVIL

A. THE METHOD OF SATYAGRAHA

1

THE CUP OF LOVE

Having flung aside the sword, there is nothing except the cup of love which I can offer to those who oppose me. It is by offering that cup that I expect to draw them close to me.

Young India, 2-4-'31

My goal is friendship with the whole world and I can combine the greatest love with the greatest opposition to wrong.

Young India, 10-3-'20

Non-violence is 'not a resignation from all real fighting against wickedness.' On the contrary, the non-violence of my conception is a more active and real fight against wickedness than retaliation whose very nature is to increase wickedness. I contemplate a mental and therefore a moral opposition to immoralities. I seek entirely to blunt the edge of the tyrant's sword, not by putting up against it a sharper-edged weapon, but by disappointing his expectation that I would be offering physical resistance. The resistance of the soul that I should offer would elude him. It would at first dazzle him and at last compel recognition from him, which recognition would not humiliate him but would uplift him.

Young India, 8-10-'25

2

SATYAGRAHA

In Satyagraha there is not the remotest idea of injuring the opponent. Satyagraha postulates the conquest of the adversary by suffering in one's own person.

Sabarmati — Report of the meeting of the Federation of International Fellowships held at Sabarmati, Jan. 13 to 15, 1928; p. 179.

The hardest heart and the grossest ignorance must disappear before the rising sun of suffering without anger and without malice.

Young India, 19-2-'25

Non-violence in its dynamic condition means conscious suffering. It does not mean meek submission to the will of the evil-doer, but it means the pitting of one's whole soul against the will of the tyrant. Working under this law of our being, it is possible for a single individual to defy the whole might of an unjust empire to save his honour, his religion, his soul and lay the foundation for that empire's fall or its regeneration.

Young India, 11-8-'20

The Satyagrahi's course is plain. He must stand unmoved in the midst of all cross currents. He may not be impatient with blind orthodoxy, nor be irritated over the unbelief of the suppressed people. He must know that his suffering will melt the stoniest heart of the stoniest fanatic. He must know that relief will come when there is least hope for it. For such is the way of the cruelly-kind Deity who insists upon testing His devotee through a fiery furnace and delights in humbling him to the dust.

Young India, 4-6-'25

3

NO ROOM FOR COWARDICE

My creed of non-violence is an extremely active force. It has no room for cowardice or even weakness. There is hope for a violent man to be some day non-violent, but there is none for a coward. I have therefore said more than once in these pages that if we do not know how to defend ourselves, our women and our places of worship by the force of suffering, i.e. non-violence, we must, if we are men, be at least able to defend all these by fighting.

Young India, 16-6-'27

There are two ways of defence. The best and the most effective is not to defend at all, but to remain at one's post risking every danger. The next best but equally honourable method is to strike bravely in self-defence and put one's life in the most dangerous positions.

Young India, 18-12-'24

Non-violence and cowardice go ill together. I can imagine a fully armed man to be at heart a coward. Possession of arms implies an element of fear, if not cowardice. But true non-violence is an impossibility without the possession of unadulterated fearlessness.

Harijan, 15-7-'39

I do believe that, where there is only a choice between cowardice and violence, I would advise violence. I would rather have India resort to arms in order to defend her honour than that she should, in a cowardly manner, become or remain a helpless witness to her own dishonour.

But I believe that non-violence is infinitely superior to violence, forgiveness is more manly than punishment. Forgiveness adorns the soldier. But abstinence is forgiveness only when there is the power to punish ; it is meaningless when it pretends to proceed from a helpless creature. But I do not believe India to be helpless. I do not believe myself to be a helpless creature. Strength does not come from physical capacity. It comes from an indomitable will.

Young India, 11-8-'20

4

NO COERCION

It is never the intention of a Satyagrahi to embarrass the wrongdoer. The appeal is never to his fear; it is, must be, always to his heart. The Satyagrahi's object is to convert, not to coerce, the wrongdoer. He should avoid artificiality in all his doings. He acts naturally and from inward conviction.

Harijan, 25-3-'39

Immediately we begin to think of things as our opponents think of them we shall be able to do them full justice. I know that this requires a detached state of mind, and it is a state very difficult to reach. Nevertheless for a Satyagrahi it is absolutely essential. Three-fourths of the miseries and misunderstandings of the world will disappear, if we step into the shoes of our adversaries and understand their standpoint. We will then agree with our adversaries quickly or think of them charitably.

I have found that mere appeal to reason does not answer where prejudices are agelong and based on supposed religious authority. Reason has to be strengthened by suffering and suffering opens the eyes of understanding. Therefore there must be no trace of compulsion in our acts. We must not be impatient; and we must have an undying faith in the means we are adopting.

Young India, 19-3-'25

Our motto must ever be conversion by gentle persuasion and a constant appeal to the head and the heart. We must therefore be ever courteous and patient with those who do not see eye to eye with us.

Young India, 29-9-'21

A Satyagrahi bids goodbye to fear. He is therefore never afraid of trusting the opponent. Even if the opponent plays him false twenty times, the Satyagrahi is ready to trust him the twentyfirst time, for an implicit trust in human nature is the very essence of his creed.

Sabarmati — Report of the meeting of the Federation of International Fellowships held at Sabarmati, 1928; p. 246.

5

HOW SATYAGRAHA GROWS IN STRENGTH

The power of suggestion is such, that a man at last becomes what he believes himself to be. If we are Satyagrahis and offer Satyagraha believing ourselves to be strong, two clear consequences result from it. Fostering the idea of strength, we grow stronger and stronger every day. With the increase in our strength our Satyagraha too becomes more effective and we would never be casting about for an opportunity to give it up.

Sabarmati, p. 178

My experience has taught me that a law of progression applies to every righteous struggle. But in the case of Satyagraha the law amounts to an axiom. As a Satyagraha struggle progresses onward, many an other element helps to swell its current, and there is a constant growth in the results to which it leads. This is really inevitable, and is bound up with the first principles of Satyagraha. For in Satyagraha the minimum is also the maximum, and as it is the irreducible minimum, there is no question of retreat, and the only movement possible is an advance. In other struggles, even when they are righteous, the demand is first pitched a little higher so as to admit of future reduction, and hence the law of progression does not apply to all of them without exception.

Sabarmati, p. 319

6

RULES FOR SATYAGRAHIS

1. There must be common honesty among Satyagrahis.

2. They must render heart discipline to their commander. There should be no mental reservation.

3. They must be prepared to lose all, not merely their personal liberty, not merely their possessions, land, cash, etc., but also the liberty and possessions of their families, and they must be ready cheerfully to face bullets, bayonets, or even slow death by torture.

4. They must not be violent in thought, word or deed towards the 'enemy' or among themselves.

Harijan, 22-10-'38

7

HUMILITY

A non-co-operator is nothing if he is not humble. He who offers a little sacrifice from a lowly and religious spirit quickly realizes the littleness of it. Once on the path of sacrifice, we find out the measure of our selfishness and must continually wish to give more and not be satisfied till there is a complete self-surrender.

Young India, 29-9-'21

8

FASTS

Fasting unto death is an integral part of Satyagraha programme, and it is the greatest and most effective weapon in its armoury under given circumstances. Not every one is qualified for undertaking it without a proper course of training.

I may not burden this note with an examination of the circumstances under which fasting may be resorted to and the training required for it. Non-violence in its positive aspect as benevolence (I do not use the word ' love ' as it has fallen into disrepute) is the greatest force because of the limitless scope it affords for self-suffering without causing or intending any physical or material injury to the wrongdoer. The object always is to evoke the best in him. Self-suffering is an appeal to his better nature, as retaliation is to his baser. Fasting under proper circumstances is such an appeal *par excellence*. If the politician does not perceive its propriety in political matters, it is because it is a novel use of this very fine weapon.

Harijan, 26-7-'42

Fast is the last weapon in the armoury of the votary of Ahimsa. When human ingenuity fails, the votary fasts. This fasting quickens the spirit of prayer, that is to say, the fasting is a spiritual act and, therefore, addressed to God. The effect of such action on the life of the people is that when the person fasting is at all known to them their sleeping conscience is awakened. But there is the danger that the people through mistaken sympathy may act against their will in order to save the life of the loved one. This danger has got to be faced. One ought not to be deterred from right action when one is sure of the rightness. It can but promote circumspection. Such a fast is undertaken in obedience to the dictates of the inner voice and therefore, prevents haste.

Harijan, 21-12-'47

9

NO SITTING DHURNA

Some students have revived the ancient form of barbarity in the form of 'sitting Dhurna'. I call it 'barbarity' for it is a crude way of using coercion. It is also cowardly because one who sits Dhurna knows that he is not going to be trampled over. It is difficult to call the practice violent, but it is certainly worse. If we fight our opponent, we at least enable him to return the blow. But when we challenge him to walk over us, we, knowing that he will not, place him in a most awkward and humiliating position. I know that the overzealous students who sat Dhurna never thought of the barbarity of the deed. But one, who is expected to follow the voice of conscience and stand even single-handed in the face of odds, cannot afford to be thoughtless. Let non-co-operationists therefore beware of everything they do. There must be no impatience, no barbarity, no insolence, no undue pressure.

Young India, 2-2-'21

10

NO COMPULSION OR INTOLERANCE

Our tyranny, if we impose our will on others, will be infinitely worse than that of the handful of Englishmen who form the bureaucracy. Theirs is a terrorism imposed by a minority struggling to exist in the midst of opposition. Ours will be a terrorism imposed by a majority and therefore worse and really more godless than the first. We must therefore eliminate compulsion in any shape from our struggle. If we are only a handful holding freely the doctrine of non-co-operation, we may have to die in the attempt to convert others to our view, but we shall have truly defended and represented our cause. If however we enlist under our banner men by force, we shall be denying our cause and God, and if we seem to succeed for the moment, we shall have succeeded in establishing a worse terror.

We shall also retard our cause if we suppress opinion by intolerance. For then we shall never know who is with us and who is against us. The indispensable condition therefore of success is that we encourage the greatest freedom of opinion. It is the least we can learn from the present 'masters'. Their Penal Code contains drastic punishments for holding opinions they do not like. And they have arrested some of the noblest of our countrymen for expression of their opinion. Our non-co-operation is a defiantly open protest against that system. We may not in the very act of fighting the restraint on opinion be guilty ourselves of imposing it on others.

***Young India*, 27-10-'21**

11

WHO IS TO OFFER SATYAGRAHA?

It is the essence of Satyagraha that those who are suffering should alone offer it. Cases can be conceived when what may be termed sympathetic Satyagraha may be legitimately applied. The idea underlying Satyagraha is to convert the wrongdoer, to awaken the sense of justice in him, to show him also that without the co-operation direct, or indirect, of the wronged the wrongdoer cannot do the wrong intended by him. If the people in either case are not ready to suffer for their causes, no outside help in the shape of Satyagraha can possibly bring true deliverance.

***Harijan*, 10-12-'38**

12

THE MANNER OF SATYAGRAHA

In a Satyagraha campaign the mode of fight and the choice of tactics, e.g. whether to advance or retreat, offer civil resistance or organize non-violent strength through constructive work and purely selfless humanitarian service, are determined according to the exigencies of the situation. A Satyagrahi must carry out whatever plan is laid out for him with a cool determination giving way to neither excitement nor depression.

Harijan, 27-5-'39

Discipline has a place in non-violent strategy, but much more is required. In a Satyagraha army everybody is a soldier and a servant. But at a pinch every Satyagrahi soldier has also to be his own general and leader. Mere discipline cannot make for leadership. The latter calls for faith and vision.

Harijan, 28-7-'40

13

NUMBERS DO NOT COUNT

In every great cause it is not the number of fighters that counts but it is the quality of which they are made that becomes the deciding factor. The greatest men of the world have always stood alone.

Young India, 10-11-'29

14

SATYAGRAHA AS THE LAST RESORT

Since Satyagraha is one of the most powerful methods of direct action, a Satyagrahi exhausts all other means before he resorts to Satyagraha. He will therefore constantly and continually approach the constituted authority, he will appeal to public opinion, educate public opinion, state his case calmly and coolly before everybody, who wants to listen to him, and only after he has exhausted all these avenues will he resort to Satyagraha. But when he has found the impelling call of the inner voice within him and launches out upon Satyagraha he has burnt his boats and there is no receding.

Young India, 20-10-'27

B. ECONOMIC INEQUALITY

1

NON-CO-OPERATION

If I would recognize the fundamental equality, as I must, of the capitalist and the labourer, I must not aim at his destruction. I must strive for his conversion. My non-co-operation with him will open his eyes to the wrong he may be doing. It can be easily demonstrated that destruction of the capitalist must mean destruction in the end of the worker; and as no human being is so bad as to be beyond redemption, no human being is so perfect as to warrant his destroying him whom he wrongly considers to be wholly evil.

Young India, 26-3-'31

There is in English a very potent word, and you have it in French also; all the languages of the world have it — it is 'No'; and the secret that we have hit upon is that when capital wants labour to say 'Yes', labour roars out 'No', if it means 'No'. And immediately labour comes to recognize that it has got its choice of saying 'Yes' when it wants to say 'Yes', and 'No' when it wants to say 'No', labour is free of capital and capital has to woo labour. And it would not matter in the slightest degree that capital has guns and even poison gas at its disposal. Capital would still be perfectly helpless if labour would assert its dignity by making good its 'No'. Labour does not need to retaliate, but labour stands defiant receiving the bullets and poison gas and still insists upon its 'No'.

The whole reason why labour so often fails is that instead of sterilizing capital, as I have suggested, labour (I am speaking as a labourer myself) wants to seize that capital and become capitalist itself in the worse sense of the term. And the capitalist, therefore, who is properly entrenched and organized, finding among labourers also candidates for the same office, makes use of a portion of these to suppress labour. If we really were not under the hypnotic spell, everyone of us, men and women, would recognize this rock-bottom truth without the slightest difficulty.

India's Case for Swaraj, p. 394

At the root of the doctrine of equal distribution must lie that of the trusteeship of the wealthy for superfluous wealth possessed by them. For according to the doctrine they may not possess a rupee more than their neighbours. How is this to be brought about? Non-violently? Or should the wealthy be dispossessed of their possessions? To do this we would naturally have to resort to violence. This violent action cannot benefit society. Society will be the poorer, for it will lose the gifts of a man who knows how to accumulate wealth. Therefore, the non-violent way is evidently superior. The rich man will be left in possession of his wealth, of which he will use what he reasonably requires for his personal needs and will act as a trustee for the remainder to be used for the society. In this argument, honesty on the part of the trustee is assumed.

If however, in spite of the utmost effort, the rich do not become guardians of the poor in the true sense of the term and the latter are more and more crushed and die of hunger, what is to be done? In trying to find out the solution of this riddle I have lighted on non-violent non-co-operation and civil disobedience as the right and infallible means. The rich cannot accumulate wealth without the co-operation of the poor in society. If this knowledge were to penetrate to and spread amongst the poor, they would become strong and would learn how to free themselves by means of non-violence from the crushing inequalities which have brought them to the verge of starvation.

Harijan, 25-8-'40

The moment the cultivators of the soil realize their power, the zamindari evil will be sterilized. What can the poor zamindar do when they say that they will simply not work the land unless they are paid enough to feed and clothe and educate themselves and their children in a decent manner. In reality the toiler is the owner of what he produces. If the toilers intelligently combine, they will become an irresistible power. That is how I do not see the necessity of class conflict. If I thought it inevitable, I should not hesitate to preach it and teach it.

Harijan, 5-12-'36

2

CLASS WAR

Class war is foreign to the essential genius of India, which is capable of evolving communism on the fundamental rights of all on equal justice. Ramarajya of my dream ensures rights alike of prince and pauper.

You may be sure that I shall throw the whole weight of my influence in preventing class war.

Socialism and communism of the West are based on certain conceptions which are fundamentally different from ours. One such conception is their belief in the essential selfishness of human nature. I do not subscribe to it for I know that the essential difference between man and the brute is that the former can respond to the call of the spirit in him, can rise superior to the passions that he owns in common with the brute and, therefore, superior to selfishness and violence, which belong to the brute nature and not to the immortal spirit of man. That is the fundamental conception of Hinduism, which has years of penance and austerity at the back of its discovery of this truth. That is why, we have had saints who have worn out their bodies and laid down their lives in order to explore the secrets of the soul. Our socialism or communism should, therefore, be based on non-violence and on harmonious co-operation of labour and capital, landlord and tenant.

***Amrit Bazar Patrika*, 2-8-'34**

In reply to a question raised by students Gandhiji said :

I would like to use the landlords and the capitalists for the service of the masses. We must not sacrifice the interests of the masses to the capitalists. We must not play their game. We must trust them to the measure of their ability to surrender their gains for the service of the masses. They are not insusceptible to the higher appeal. It has been my invariable experience that a kind word uttered, goes home to them. If we win their confidence and put them at their ease, we will find that they are not averse to progressively sharing their riches with the masses.

Moreover, let us ask ourselves how much we have done to identify ourselves with the masses. Have we bridged the gulf between the surging millions and us ? Let us, who live in glass houses, not throw stones. To what extent do you share the life of the masses ? I confess that with me, it is still an aspiration. We ourselves have not completely shed the habits of living that we say that the capitalists are notorious for.

The idea of class war does not appeal to me. In India a class war is not only not inevitable, but it is avoidable if we have understood the message of non-violence. Those who talk about class war as being inevitable, have not understood the implications of non-violence or have understood them only skin-deep.

Let us not be obsessed with catchwords and seductive slogans imported from the West. Have we not our distinct Eastern tradition? Are we not capable of finding our own solution to the question of capital and labour? What is the system of Varnashrama but a means of harmonizing the difference between high and low, as well as between capital and labour? All that comes from the West on this subject is tarred with the brush of violence. I object to it because I have seen the wreckage that lies at the end of this road. The more thinking set even in the West today stand aghast at the abyss for which their system is heading. And I owe whatever influence I have in the West to my ceaseless endeavour to find a solution which promises an escape from the vicious circle of violence and exploitation. I have been a sympathetic student of the Western social order and I have discovered that underlying the fever that fills the soul of the West there is a restless search for truth. I value that spirit. Let us study our Eastern institutions in that spirit of scientific enquiry and we shall evolve a truer socialism and a truer communism than the world has yet dreamed of. It is surely wrong to presume that Western socialism or communism is the last word on the question of mass poverty.

Amrit Bazar Patrika, 3-8-'34

The problem is not to set class against class, but to educate labour to a sense of its dignity. Moneyed men after all form a microscopic minority in the world. They will act on the square, immediately labour realizes its power and yet acts on the square. To inflame labour against moneyed men is to perpetuate class hatred and all the evil consequences flowing from it. The strife is a vicious circle to be avoided at any cost. It is an admission of weakness, a sign of inferiority complex. The moment labour recognizes its own dignity, money will find its rightful place, i.e. it will be held in trust for labour. For labour is more than money.

Harijan, 16-10-'45

I do not teach the masses to regard the capitalists as their enemies, but I teach them that they are their own enemies.

Young India, 26-11-'31

3

LABOUR ORGANIZATION

NEED FOR ORGANIZING LABOUR

Speaking to workmen Gandhiji remarked that what he had been saying for years was that labour was far superior to capital. He wanted marriage between capital and labour. They could work wonders in co-operation. But that could happen only when labour was intelligent enough to co-operate with itself and then offer co-operation with capital on terms of honourable equality. Capital controlled labour because it knew the art of combination. Drops in separation could only fade away; drops in co-operation made the ocean which carried on its broad bosom ocean greyhounds. Similarly, if all the labourers in any part of the world combined together they could not be tempted by higher wages or helplessly allow themselves to be attracted for, say, a pittance. A true and non-violent combination of labour would act like a magnet attracting to it all the needed capital. Capitalists would then exist only as trustees. When that happy day dawned, there would be no difference between capital and labour. Then labour will have ample food, good and sanitary dwellings, all the necessary education for their children, ample leisure for self-education and proper medical assistance.

Harijan, 7-9-'47

One word about policy. It is not anti-capitalistic. The idea is to take from capital labour's due share and no more, and this, not by paralyzing capital, but by reform among labourers from within and by their own self-consciousness; not again through the cleverness and manoeuvring of non-labour leaders, but by educating labour to evolve its own leadership and its own self-reliant, self-existing organization. Its direct aim is not in the least degree political. Its direct aim is internal reform and evolution of internal strength. The indirect result of this evolution when, and if it ever becomes complete, will naturally be tremendously political.

I have not, therefore, the remotest idea of exploiting labour or organizing it for any direct political power of first-class importance when it becomes a self-existing unit. Labour, in my opinion, must not become a pawn in the hands of the politician on the political chessboard. It must, by its sheer strength, dominate the chessboard.

From a letter dated May 10, '27 in *Is India Different?*: Being correspondence between S. Saklatwala and Gandhiji; published by the Communist Party of Great Britain, 16, King Street, London; 1927; p. 25.

SUBSIDIARY OCCUPATIONS FOR MILL-HANDS

A mill-hand's life is ever full of vicissitudes. Thrift and economy no doubt provide a sort of remedy and it would be criminal to neglect them. But the saving thus made cannot carry one far, seeing that the vast bulk of our mill labourers are always struggling on the margin of bare subsistence. Moreover it would never do for a working man during strike or unemployment to rest idly at home. There is nothing more injurious to his morale and self-respect than enforced idleness. The working class will never feel secure or develop a sense of self-assurance and strength unless its members are armed with an unfailing subsidiary means of subsistence to serve as a second string to their bow in a crisis.

The idea of a subsidiary occupation for the mill-hands was first conceived by me during the eventful twentythree days' strike of the Ahmedabad mill-hands in the year 1918. It occurred to me then that if the strike was to be successful the mill-hands must have an occupation that would maintain them wholly or partly. They must not rely upon doles. During the strike many of them were employed on unskilled labour. It was then that I mooted my suggestion to teach mill-hands a subsidiary occupation. But my suggestion remained a dead letter till the next strike came. A sort of a beginning was made then. But it was difficult to bring into being all of a sudden an effective organization for teaching subsidiary occupations. With the end of the second strike died also the effort to find and teach suitable occupations.

An organized and systematic effort is now being made by the Labour Union (of Ahmedabad) in that direction. Mill-hands are being taught to select occupations which they can practise in their leisure hours at home and which would give them substantial relief in times of unemployment. These are ginning, cleaning, carding and spinning of cotton, weaving, tailoring, soap and paper making, type-setting, etc.

I hold that a working knowledge of a variety of occupations is to the working class what metal is to the capitalist. But the difficulty is that whilst today capital is organized and seems to be securely entrenched. labour is not. The intelligence of the working man is cramped by his soulless, mechanical occupation which leaves him little scope or chance to develop his mind. It has prevented him from realizing the power and full dignity of his status. He has been taught to believe that his wages have to be dictated by capitalists instead of his demanding his own terms. Let him only be organized along right lines and have his intelligence quickened, let him learn a variety of occupations, and he will be able to go about with his head erect and never be afraid of being without means of sustenance.

Harijan, 3-7-'37

4

STATE ACTION

CONFISCATION BY LEGISLATION

I am afraid that for years to come India would be engaged in passing legislation in order to raise the down-trodden, the fallen, from the mire into which they have been sunk by the capitalists, by the landlords, by the so-called higher classes, and then, subsequently and scientifically, by the British rulers. If we are to lift these people from the mire, then it would be the bounden duty of the National Government of India, in order to set its house in order, continually to give preference to these people and even free them from the burdens under which they are being crushed. And, if the landlords, zamindars, moneyed men and those who are today enjoying privileges — I do not care whether they are Europeans or Indians — if they find that they are discriminated against, I shall sympathize with them, but I will not be able to help them, even if I could possibly do so, because I would seek their assistance in that process, and without their assistance it would not be possible to raise these people out of the mire.

Look at the condition, if you will, of the 'un-touchables', if the law comes to their assistance and sets apart miles of territory. At the present moment they hold no land; they are absolutely living at the mercy of the so-called higher castes, and also, let me say, at the mercy of the State. They can be removed from one quarter to another without complaint and without being able to seek the assistance of law. Well, the first act of the legislature will then be to see that in order somewhat to equalize conditions, these people are given grants freely.

From whose pockets are those grants to come? Not from the pockets of Heaven. Heaven is not going to drop money for the sake of the State. They will naturally come from the moneyed classes, including the Europeans.

I have got another formula also, hurriedly drafted because I drafted it here as I was listening to Lord Reading and Sir Tej Bahadur Sapru. It is in connection with existing rights :

> "No existing interest legitimately acquired and not being in conflict with the best interests of the nation in general, shall be interfered with except in accordance with the law applicable to such interests."

I certainly have in mind what you find in the Congress resolution in connection with the taking over by the incoming Government of obligations that are being today discharged by the British Government. Just as we claim that these obligations must be examined by an impartial tribunal before they are taken over by us, so should existing interests be subject to judicial scrutiny when necessary. There is no question, therefore, of repudiation but merely of taking over under examination under audit. We have here some of us who have made a study of the privileges and monopolies enjoyed by the Europeans, but let it not be merely Europeans : there are Indians — I have undoubtedly several Indians in mind — who are today in possession of land which has been practically given away to them not for any service rendered to the nation but for some service rendered, I cannot even say to the Government, because I do not think that the Government has benefited, but to some official ; and if you tell me that those concessions and those privileges are not to be examined by the State, I again tell you that it will be impossible to run the machinery of Government on behalf of the have-nots, on behalf of the dispossessed. Hence, you will see that there is nothing stated here in connection with the Europeans. The second formula also is applicable equally to the Europeans as it is applicable to Indians, as it is applicable, say, to Sir Purushottamdas Thakurdas and Sir Pheroze Sethna. If they have obtained concessions which have been obtained because they did some service to the officials of the day and got some miles of land, well, if I had the possession of the Government I would quickly dispossess them. I would not consider them because they are Indians, and I would just as readily dispossess Sir Hubert Carr or Mr. Benthall, however admirable they are and however friendly they are to me. The law will be no respecter of persons whatsoever. I give you that assurance. I am unable to go any further. So, that is really what is implied by 'legitimately acquired'—that every interest must have been taintless, it must be above suspicion, like Caesar's wife, and therefore, we shall expect to examine all these things when they come under the notice of the Government.

Then you have 'not being in conflict with the best interests of the nation'. I have in mind certain monopolies legitimately acquired, undoubtedly, but which have been brought into being in conflict with the best interests of the nation. Let me give you an illustration which will amuse you somewhat, but which is on natural ground. Take this white elephant which is called New Delhi. Crores have been spent upon it. Suppose that the future Government comes to the conclusion that seeing that we have got this white elephant it ought to be turned to some use. Imagine that in Old Delhi there is a plague or cholera going on, and we want hospitals for the poor people. What are we to do? Do you suppose that the National Government will be able to build hospitals, and so on? Nothing of the kind. We will take charge of those buildings and put these plague-stricken people in them and use them as hospitals, because I contend that those buildings are in conflict with the best interests of the nation. They do not represent the millions of India. They may be representative of the moneyed men who are sitting here at the table; they may be representative of His Highness the Nawab Sahib of Bhopal, or of Sir Purushottamdas Thakurdas, or of Sir Pheroze Sethna, or of Sir Tej Bahadur Sapru, but they are not representative of those who lack even a place to sleep and have not even a crust of bread to eat. If the National Government comes to the conclusion that that place is unnecessary, no matter what interests are concerned, they will be dispossessed, and they will be dispossessed, I may tell you, without any compensation, because, if you want this Government to pay compensation it will have to rob Peter and pay Paul, and that would be impossible.

It is a bitter pill which has got to be swallowed if a Government, as Congress conceives it, comes into being.

[From a speech before the Round Table Conference in London]
The Nation's Voice, 1932; p. 71

C. SOCIAL DISORDER

1

RIOTS

PEACE BRIGADE

To quell riots non-violently, there must be true Ahimsa in one's heart, an Ahimsa that takes even the erring hooligan in its warm embrace. Such an attitude has to be cultivated. It can only come as a result of prolonged and patient effort which must be made during peaceful times. The would-be member of a peace brigade should come into close touch and cultivate acquaintance with the so-called *goonda* element in his vicinity. He should know all and be known to all and win the hearts of all by his loving and selfish service. No section should be regarded as too contemptible or mean to mix with. *Goondas* do not drop from the sky, nor do they spring from the earth like evil spirits. They are the product of social disorganization, and society is therefore responsible for their existence. In other words, they should be looked upon as a symptom of corruption in our body politic. To remove the disease we must first discover the underlying cause. To find the remedy will then be a comparatively easy task.

Harijan, 15-9-'40

Let no one understand from the foregoing that a non-violent army (Peace Brigade) is open only to those who strictly enforce in their lives all the implications of non-violence. It is open to all those who accept the implications and make an ever-increasing endeavour to observe them. There never will be an army of perfectly non-violent people. It will be formed of those who will honestly endeavour to observe non-violence.

Harijan, 21-7-'40

A non-violent army (Peace Brigade) acts unlike armed men, as well in times of peace as of disturbances. They would be constantly engaged in constructive activities that make riots impossible. Theirs will be the duty of seeking occasions for bringing warring communities together, carrying on peace propaganda, engaging in activities that would bring and keep them in touch with every single person, male and female, adult and child, in their parish or division. Such an army should be ready to cope with any emergency, and in order to still the frenzy of mobs should risk their lives in numbers sufficient for the purpose. A few hundred, may be a few thousand, such spotless deaths will once for all put an end to the riots. Surely a few hundred young men and women giving themselves deliberately to mob fury will be any day a cheap and braver method of dealing with such madness than the display and use of the police and the military.

Harijan, 26-3-'38

Some time ago I suggested the formation of a Peace Brigade whose members would risk their lives in dealing with riots, especially communal. The idea was that this Brigade should substitute the police and even the military.

Let us therefore see what qualifications a member of the contemplated Peace Brigade should possess :

1. He or she must have a living faith in non-violence. This is impossible without a living faith in God. A non-violent man can do nothing save by the power and grace of God. Without it he would not have the courage to die without anger, without fear and without retaliation. Such courage comes from the belief that God sits in the hearts of all and that there should be no fear in the presence of God. The knowledge of the omnipresence of God also

means respect for the lives of even those who may be called opponents or *goondas*. This contemplated intervention is a process of stilling the fury of man when the brute in him gets the mastery over him.

2. This messenger of peace must have equal regard for all the principal religions of the earth. Thus, if he is a Hindu, he will respect the other faiths current in India. He must therefore possess a knowledge of the general principles of the different faiths professed in the country.

3. Generally speaking this work of peace can only be done by local men in their own localities.

4. The work can be done singly or in groups. Therefore no one need wait for companions. Nevertheless one would naturally seek companions in one's own locality and form a local Brigade.

5. This messenger of peace will cultivate through personal service contacts with the people in his locality or chosen circle, so that when he appears to deal with ugly situations, he does not descend upon the members of a riotous assembly as an utter stranger liable to be looked upon as a suspect or an unwelcome visitor.

6. Needless to say, a peace bringer must have a character beyond reproach and must be known for his strict impartiality.

7. Generally there are previous warnings of coming storms. If these are known, the Peace Brigade will not wait till the conflagration breaks out but will try to handle the situation in anticipation.

8. Whilst, if the movement spreads, it might be well if there are some whole-time workers, it is not absolutely necessary that there should be. The idea is to have as many good and true men and women as possible. These can be had only if volunteers are drawn from those who are engaged in various walks of life but have leisure enough to cultivate friendly relations with the people living in their circles and otherwise possess the qualifications required of a member of the Peace Brigade.

9. There should be a distinctive dress worn by the members of the contemplated Brigade so that in course of

time they will be recognized without the slightest difficulty.

These are but general suggestions. Each centre can work out its own constitution on the basis here suggested.

Harijan, 18-6-'38

Some time ago an attempt was made, at my instance, to form Shanti Dal (Peace Brigades) but nothing came of it. This lesson, however, was learnt that the membership, in its very nature, of such organizations could not be large. Ordinarily, the efficient running of a large volunteer corps based on force implies the possibility of the use of force in the event of breach of discipline. In such bodies little or no stress is laid on a man's character. Physique is the chief factor. The contrary must obtain in non-violent bodies in which character or soul force must mean everything and physique must take second place. It is difficult to find many such persons. That is why non-violent corps must be small, if they are to be efficient. Such Brigades may be scattered all over ; there may be one each for a village or a Mohalla. The members must know one another well. Each corps will select its own head. All the members will have the same status, but where everyone is doing the same work there must be one person under whose discipline all must come, or else the work will suffer. Where there are two or more Brigades the leaders must consult among themselves and decide on a common line of action. In that way alone lies success.

If non-violent volunteer corps are formed on the above lines, they can easily stop trouble. These corps will not require all the physical training given in Akhadas, but a certain part of it will be necessary.

One thing, however, should be common to members of all such organizations and that is implicit faith in God. He is the only companion and doer. Without faith in Him these Peace Brigades will be lifeless. By whatever name one calls God, one must realize that one can only work through His strength. Such a man will never take another's life. He will allow himself, if need be, to be killed and thereby live through his victory over death.

The mind of the man in whose life the realization of this law has become a living reality will not be bewildered in crisis. He will instinctively know the right way to act.

In spite, however, of what I have said above, I would like to give some rules culled from my own experience:

1. A volunteer may not carry any weapons.
2. The members of a corps must be easily recognizable.
3. Every volunteer must carry bandages, scissors, needle and thread, surgical knife, etc. for rendering first aid.
4. He should know how to carry and remove the wounded.
5. He should know how to put out fires, how to enter a fire area without getting burnt, how to climb heights for rescue work and descend safely with or without his charge.
6. He should be well acquainted with all the residents of his locality. This is a service in itself.
7. He should recite Ramanama ceaselessly in his heart and persuade others who believe to do likewise.

Man often repeats the name of God parrot-wise and expects fruit from so doing. The true seeker must have that living faith which will not only dispel the untruth of parrot-wise repetition from within him but also from the hearts of others.

Harijan, 5-5-'46

AGAINST COMMUNAL KILLINGS

Murder can never be avenged by either murder or taking compensation. The only way to avenge murder is to offer oneself as a willing sacrifice, with no desire for retaliation. Revenge or compensation may furnish some satisfaction to the individual, but I am quite definite that it can never restore peace to or uplift society.

Harijan, 18-8-'46

POLICE FORCE

Even in a non-violent State a police force may be necessary. This, I admit, is a sign of my imperfect Ahimsa. I have not the courage to declare that we can carry on without a police force as I have in respect of an army. Of course

I can and do envisage a State where the police will not be necessary; but whether we shall succeed in realizing it, the future alone will show.

The police of my conception will, however, be of a wholly different pattern from the present-day force. Its ranks will be composed of believers in non-violence. They will be servants, not masters, of the people. The people will instinctively render them every help, and through mutual co-operation they will easily deal with the ever-decreasing disturbances. The police force will have some kind of arms, but they will be rarely used, if at all. In fact the policemen will be reformers. Their police work will be confined primarily to robbers and dacoits. Quarrels between labour and capital and strikes will be few and far between in a non-violent State, because the influence of the non-violent majority will be so great as to command the respect of the principal elements in society. Similarly there will be no room for communal disturbances.

Harijan, 1-9-'40

2

THEFTS

A well-armed man has stolen your property; you have harboured the thought of his act; you are filled with anger; you argue that you want to punish that rogue, not for your own sake, but for the good of your neighbours; you have collected a number of armed men, you want to take his house by assault; he is duly informed of it, he runs away; he too is incensed. He collects his brother robbers, and sends you a defiant message that he will commit robbery in broad daylight. You are strong, you do not fear him. you are prepared to receive him. Meanwhile, the robber pesters your neighbours. They complain before you. You reply that you are doing all for their sake, you do not mind that your own goods have been stolen. Your neighbours reply that the robber never pestered them before, and that he commenced his depredations only after you declared hostilities against him. You are between Scylla and Charybdis. You are full of pity for the poor men. What they say is true. What are you to do ? You will be disgraced if you now leave the robber alone. You, therefore, tell the poor men : "Never mind. Come, my wealth is yours, I will give you arms, I will teach you how to use them ; you should belabour the rogue ; don't you leave him alone." And so the battle grows ; the robbers increase in numbers ; your neighbours have deliberately put themselves to inconvenience. Thus the result of wanting to take revenge upon the robber is that you have disturbed your own peace ; you are in perpetual fear of being robbed and assaulted ; your courage has given place to cowardice. If you will patiently examine the argument, you will see that I have not overdrawn the picture. This is one of the means.

Now let us examine the other. You set this armed robber down as an ignorant brother ; you intend to reason with him at a suitable opportunity ; you argue that he is, after all, a fellow man ; you do not know what prompted him to steal. You, therefore, decide that, when you can, you will destroy the man's motive for stealing. Whilst you are thus reasoning with yourself, the man comes again to steal. Instead of being angry with him you take pity on him. You think that this stealing habit must be a disease with him. Henceforth, you, therefore, keep your doors and windows open, you change your sleeping-place, and you keep your things in a manner most accessible to him. The robber comes again and is confused as all this is new to him ; nevertheless, he takes away your things. But his mind is agitated. He inquires about you in the village, he comes to learn about your broad and loving heart, he repents, he begs your pardon, returns you your things, and leaves off the stealing habit. He becomes your servant. and you find for him honourable employment. This is the second method. Thus, you see, different means have brought about totally different results. I do not wish to deduce from this that robbers will act in the above manner or that all will have the same pity and love like you, but I only wish to show that fair means alone can produce fair results, and that, at least in the majority of cases, if not indeed in all, the force of love and pity is infinitely greater than the force of arms. There is harm in the exercise of brute force, never in that of pity.

Hind Swaraj, 1946, written in 1908; pp. 53, 54

Q. What is the employer to do when an employee of his is addicted to stealing and is not amenable to correction whether it is by way of entreaty or the cane ?

A. My advice to the employer will be to remove all temptations in the way of the thief, to treat him as if he was his own brother and, when he refuses to yield to any treatment, however humanitarian it may be, to ask him to go his way. Let the employer always ask himself whether he would treat his own brother in the same way at the given stage.

Harijan, 21-7-'46

Speaking after the evening prayer at Uruli, Gandhiji said that instead of bearing ill-will towards a thief or a criminal and trying to get him punished they should try to get under his skin, understand the cause that had led him into crime and try to remedy it. They should, for instance, teach him a vocation and provide him with the means to make an honest living and thereby transform his life. They should realize that a thief or a criminal was not a different being from themselves. Indeed, if they turned the searchlight inward and closely looked into their own souls, they would find that the difference between them was only one of degree.

Harijan, 11-8-'46

3

ASSAULTS ON WOMEN

Where there is a non-violent atmosphere, where there is the constant teaching of Ahimsa, woman will not regard herself as dependent, weak or helpless. She is not really helpless when she is pure. Her purity makes her conscious of her strength. I have always held that it is physically impossible to violate a woman against her will. The outrage takes place only when she gives way to fear or does not realize her moral strength. If she cannot meet the assailant's physical might, her purity will give her the strength to die before he succeeds in violating her. Take the case of Sita. Physically she was a weakling before Ravana, but her purity was more than a match even for his giant might. He tried to win her with all kinds of allurements but could not carnally touch her without her consent. On the other hand, if a woman depends on her own physical strength or upon a weapon she possesses, she is sure to be discomfited whenever her strength is exhausted.

The brother or father or friend will stand between his protegee and her assailant. He will then either dissuade the assailant from his wicked purpose or allow himself to be killed by him in preventing him. In so laying down his life he will not only have done his duty, but given a new accession of strength to his protegee who will now know how to protect her honour.

Harijan, 1-9-'40

It is my firm conviction that a fearless woman who knows that her purity is her best shield can never be dishonoured. However beastly the man, he will bow in shame before the flame of her dazzling purity. There are examples even in modern times of women who have thus defended themselves. I can, as I write, recall two such instances. I therefore recommend women who read this article to try to cultivate this courage. They will become wholly fearless, if they can and cease to tremble as they do today at the thought of assaults. Parents and husbands should instruct women in the art of becoming fearless. It can best be learnt from a living faith in God. Though He is invisible, He is one's unfailing protector. He who has this faith is the most fearless of all.

But such faith or courage cannot be acquired in a day. Meantime we must try to explore other means. When a woman is assaulted she may not stop to think in terms of Himsa or Ahimsa. Her primary duty is self-protection. She is at liberty to employ every method or means that come to her mind in order to defend her honour. God has given her nails and teeth. She must use them with all her strength and, if need be, die in the effort. The man or woman who has shed all fear of death will be able not only to protect himself or herself but others also through laying down his life.

So much for what a woman should do. But what about a man who is witness to such crimes? The answer is implied in the foregoing. He must not be a passive onlooker. He must protect the woman. He must not run for police help; he must not rest satisfied by pulling the alarm chain in the train. If he is able to practise non-violence, he will die in doing so and thus save the woman in jeopardy. If he does not believe in non-violence or cannot practise it, he must try to save her by using all the force he may have. In either way there must be readiness on his part to lay down his life.

Harijan, 1-3-'42

D. POLITICAL EVILS

1

AN EVIL STATE

CIVIL DISOBEDIENCE

An out-and-out civil resister simply ignores the authority of the State. He becomes an outlaw claiming to disregard every unmoral State law. Thus for instance, he may refuse to pay taxes, he may refuse to recognize the authority of the State in his daily intercourse. He may refuse to obey the law of trespass and claim to enter military barracks in order to speak to the soldiers, he may refuse to submit to limitations upon the manner of picketing and may picket within the prescribed area. In doing all this he never uses force and never resists force when it is used against him. In fact, he invites imprisonment and other uses of force against himself. This he does because and when he finds the bodily freedom he seemingly enjoys, to be an intolerable burden. He argues to himself that a State allows personal freedom only in so far as the citizen submits to its regulations. Submission to the State law is the price a citizen pays for his personal liberty. Submission, therefore, to a State law wholly or largely unjust is an immoral barter for liberty. A citizen who thus realizes the evil nature of a State is not satisfied to live on its sufferance, and therefore appears to the others who do not share his belief to be a nuisance to society whilst he is endeavouring to compel the State, without committing a moral breach, to arrest him. Thus considered, civil resistance is a most powerful expression of a soul's anguish and an eloquent protest against the continuance of an evil State. And as a civil resistance army is or ought to be free from passion because free from the spirit of retaliation, it requires the fewest number of soldiers. Indeed one *perfect* civil resister is enough to win the battle of Right against Wrong.

***Young India*, 10-11-'21**

Those only can take up civil disobedience, who believe in willing obedience even to irksome laws imposed by the State so long as they do not hurt their conscience or religion, and are prepared equally willingly to suffer the penalty of civil disobedience. Disobedience to be civil has to be absolutely non-violent, the underlying principle being the winning over of the opponent by suffering i.e. love.

Young India, 3-11-'21

CIVIL DISOBEDIENCE IN SPITE OF VIOLENCE

A call may come which one dare not neglect, cost what it may. I can clearly see the time coming to me when I must refuse obedience to every single State-made law, even though there may be a certainty of bloodshed. When neglect of the call means a denial of God, civil disobedience becomes a peremptory duty.

Young India, 4-8-'21

Whenever I have suspended civil disobedience, I have done so, not by reason of any outbreak of violence but upon the discovery of such violence as had been initiated or encouraged by Congressmen who should have known better. Any outbreak of violence would not have brought about suspension, for instance, the Moplah outbreak. But Chauri Chaura did, for the simple reason that persons connected with the Congress were involved in it.

Young India, 29-10-'25

NON-PAYMENT OF TAXES

We must not resort to non-payment because of the possibility of a ready response. The readiness is a fatal temptation. Such non-payment will not be civil or non-violent, but it will be criminal and fraught with the greatest possibility of violence. Not until the peasantry is trained to understand the reason and the virtue of civil non-payment and is prepared to look with calm resignation upon the confiscation of their holdings and the forced sale of their cattle and other belongings, may they be advised to withhold payment of taxes.

Young India, 26-1-'22

IMPRISONMENT

A Satyagrahi goes to prison, not to embarrass the authorities but to convert them by demonstrating to them his innocence. You should realize that unless you have developed the moral fitness to go to prison, which the law of Satyagraha demands, your jail-going will be useless and will bring you nothing but disappointment in the end.

Harijan, 5-11-'38

CAN THE MASSES REMAIN NON-VIOLENT?

Q. How do you think that the masses can practise non-violence, when we know that they are all prone to anger, hate, ill-will? They are known to fight for the most trivial things.

A. They are, and yet I think they can practise non-violence for the common good. Do you think that the thousands of women that collected contraband salt had ill-will against anyone? They knew that the Congress or Gandhi had asked them to do certain things, and they did those things in faith and hope. Their belief in non-violence was unintelligent, even as the belief in the earth being round with many is unintelligent. But their belief in their leaders was genuine, and that was enough. With those who lead it is another matter. Their belief has got to be intelligent, and they have to live up to all the implications of the belief.

Harijan, 4-11-'39

2

EXTERNAL AGGRESSION

ARMS OR NO ARMS

Under Swaraj of my dream there is no necessity for arms at all. But I do not expect that dream to materialize in its fulness as a result of the present effort, first because the present effort is not directed to that end as an immediate goal, and secondly because I do not consider myself advanced enough to be able to prescribe a detailed course of conduct to the nation for such preparation. I am still myself too full of passion and other frailties of human nature to feel the call or the capacity. And therefore, it is not possible for me to show the nation a present way to complete non-violence, in practice.

Young India, 17-11-'21

CAN AGGRESSION BE STOPPED BY NON-VIOLENCE?

There are two ways in common between soldiers of war and soldiers of non-violence, and if I had been a citizen of Switzerland and a President of the Federal State what I would have done would be to refuse passage to the invading army by refusing all supplies. Secondly, by re-enacting a Thermopylae in Switzerland, you would have presented a living wall of men and women and children inviting the invaders to walk over your corpses. You may say that such a thing is beyond human experience and endurance. I say that it is not so. It was quite possible. Last year in Gujarat, women stood Lathi charges unflinchingly and in Peshawar thousands stood hails of bullets without resorting to violence. Imagine these men and women staying in front of an army requiring a safe passage to another country. The army would be brutal enough to walk over them, you might say. I would then say you will still have done your duty by allowing yourselves to be annihilated. An army that dares to pass over the corpses of innocent men and women would not be able to repeat that experiment. You may, if you wish, refuse to believe in such courage on the part of the masses of men and women; but then you would have to admit that non-violence is made of sterner stuff. It was never conceived as a weapon of the weak, but of the stoutest hearts.

Young India, 31-12-'31

Q. There is a report about some new scheme that you want to propound in one of your *Harijan* articles about non-violent non-co-operation if any invader came to India. Could you give us an idea?

A. It is wrong. I have no plan in mind. If I had, I should give it to you. But I think nothing more need be added when I have said that there should be unadulterated non-violent non-co-operation and if the whole of India responded and unanimously offered it, I should show that without shedding a single drop of blood, Japanese arms — or any combination of arms — can be sterilized. That involves the determination of India not to give quarter on any point whatsoever and to be ready to risk loss of several million lives. But I would consider that cost very cheap and victory won at that cost glorious. That India may not be ready to pay that price may be true. I hope it is not true, but some such price must be paid by any country that wants to retain its independence. After all, the sacrifice made by the Russians and the Chinese is enormous, and they are ready to risk all. The same could be said of the other countries also, whether aggressors or defenders. The cost is enormous. Therefore, in the non-violent technique I am asking India to risk no more than other countries are risking and which India would have to risk even if she offered armed resistance.

Harijan, 24-5-'42

SECTION SEVEN: WORKERS AND WORK PROGRAMME

A. THE WORKER

1

QUALIFICATIONS OF A SARVODAYA WORKER

[The following are some qualifications prescribed by Gandhiji for Satyagrahis. But as a Sarvodaya worker was, according to him, also to be a true Satyagrahi, these qualifications may be regarded as applying also to a Sarvodaya worker. — Ed.]

1. He must have a living faith in God, for He is his only Rock.

2. He must believe in truth and non-violence as his creed and therefore have faith in the inherent goodness of human nature which he expects to evoke by his truth and love expressed through his suffering.

3. He must be leading a chaste life and be ready and willing for the sake of his cause to give up his life and his possessions.

4. He must be a habitual Khadi-wearer and spinner. This is essential for India.

5. He must be a teetotaller and be free from the use of other intoxicants in order that his reason may be always unclouded and his mind constant.

6. He must carry out with a willing heart all the rules of discipline as may be laid down from time to time.

The qualifications are not to be regarded as exhaustive. They are illustrative only.

Harijan, 25-3-'39

HUMILITY

If we shatter the chains of egotism, and melt into the ocean of humanity, we share its dignity. To feel that we are something is to set up a barrier between God and ourselves ; to cease feeling that we are something is to become one with God. A drop in the ocean partakes of the greatness of its parent, although it is unconscious of it. But it is dried up, as soon as it enters upon an existence independent of the ocean.

A life of service must be one of humility. He who would sacrifice his life for others has hardly time to reserve for himself a place in the sun.

From Yeravda Mandir, 1945; pp. 46, 47

CEASELESS ACTIVITY

True humility means most strenuous and constant endeavour entirely directed towards the service of humanity. God is continuously in action without resting for a single moment. If we would serve Him or become one with Him, our activity must be as unwearied as His. There may be momentary rest in store for the drop which is separated from the ocean, but not for the drop in the ocean, which knows no rest. The same is the case with ourselves. As soon as we become one with the ocean in the shape of God, there is no more rest for us, nor indeed do we need rest any longer. Our very sleep is action. For we sleep with the thought of God in our hearts. This restlessness constitutes true rest. This never-ceasing agitation holds the key to peace ineffable.

From Yeravda Mandir, 1945; pp. 47, 48

SILENCE

Silence is part of the spiritual discipline of the votary of truth. Proneness to exaggerate, to suppress or modify the truth, willingly or unwillingly, is a natural weakness of man, and silence is necessary in order to surmount it. A man of few words will rarely be thoughtless in his speech: he will measure every word.

Autobiography, 1940; p. 84

CHASTITY

No worker who has not overcome lust can hope to render any genuine service to the cause of Harijans, communal unity, Khadi, cow-protection or village reconstruction. Great causes like these cannot be served by intellectual equipment alone, they call for spiritual effort or soul-force. Soul-force comes only through God's grace, and God's grace never descends upon a man who is a slave to lust.

Harijan, 21-11-'36

FAITH

You should be pioneers in presenting a living faith to the world, and not the dry bones of a traditional faith which the world will not grasp.

With Gandhiji in Ceylon, 1928; p. 112

Nothing great in this world was ever accomplished without a living faith.

Harijan, 9-10-'37

IDENTIFICATION WITH THE MASSES

We must first come in living touch with them (the masses) by working for them and in their midst. We must share their sorrows, understand their difficulties and anticipate their wants. With the Pariahs we must be Pariahs and see how we feel to clean the closets of the upper classes and have the remains of their table thrown at us. We must see how we like being in the boxes, miscalled houses, of the labourers of Bombay. We must identify ourselves with the villagers who toil under the hot sun beating on their bent backs and see how we would like to drink water from the pool in which the villagers bathe, wash their clothes and pots and in which their cattle drink and roll. Then and not till then shall we truly represent the masses and they will, as surely as I am writing this, respond to every call.

Young India, 11-9-'24

The golden rule to apply is resolutely to refuse to have what the millions cannot. The ability to refuse will not descend upon us all of a sudden. The first thing is to cultivate the mental attitude that we will not have possessions or facilities denied to millions, and the next immediate thing is to rearrange our lives as fast as possible in accordance with that mentality. Without a large, very large, army of such self-sacrificing and determined workers, real progress of the masses I hold to be an impossibility.

Young India, 24-6-'26

Socialism begins with the first convert. If there is one such you can add zeroes to the one and the first zero will account for ten and every addition will account for ten times the previous number. If, however, the beginner is a zero, in other words, no one makes the beginning, multiplicity of zeroes will also produce zero value. Time and paper occupied in writing zeroes will be so much waste.

Harijan, 13-7-'47

VOLUNTARY POVERTY

They (Sarvodaya workers) must learn the art and the beauty of self-denial and voluntary poverty. They must engage themselves in nation-building activities, the spread of Khaddar through personal hand-spinning and hand-weaving, the spread of communal unity of hearts by irreproachable personal conduct towards one another in every walk of life, the banishing of untouchability in every shape or form in one's own person, the spread of total abstinence from intoxicating drinks and drugs by personal contact with individual addicts, and generally by cultivating personal purity. These are services which provide maintenance on the poor man's scale. Those for whom the poor man's scale is not feasible should find a place in small unorganized industries of national importance which give a better wage.

Amrit Bazar Patrika, 8-4-'34

The detailed constructive programme is to be found in my pamphlet * on it, and Dr. Rajendra Prasad's † which is a running commentary on it. It should be remembered that it is illustrative, not exhaustive. Local circumstances may suggest many more items not touched in the printed programme. These are beyond the scope of a treatise on an All India programme. They are necessarily for local workers to find out and do the needful.

In these hints I have singled out some items ‡ for fuller emphasis in the light of experience gained since the publication of the programme.

1

KISAN

The Kisan or the peasant, whether as a landless labourer or a labouring proprietor, comes first. He is the salt of the earth which rightly belongs or should belong to him, not to the absentee landlord or zamindar. But in the non-violent way the labourer cannot forcibly eject the absentee landlord. He has so to work as to make it impossible for the landlord to exploit him. Closest co-operation amongst the peasants is absolutely necessary.

---

* *Constructive Programme, Its Meaning and Place*, Price As. 6, Postage etc., As. 3, Navajivan Publishing House, Ahmedabad-9.

† *Constructive Programme, Some Suggestions*, Price As. 8, Postage etc., As. 3, Navajivan Publishing House, Ahmedabad-9.

‡ The items listed in the pamphlet are: 1. Communal Unity; 2. Removal of Untouchability; 3. Prohibition; 4. Khadi; 5. Other Village Industries; 6. Village Sanitation; 7. Basic Education; 8. Adult Education; 9. Women; 10. Education in Health and Hygiene; 11. Provincial Languages; 12. National Language; 13. Economic Equality; 14. Kisans; 15. Labour; 16. Adivasis; 17. Lepers; 18. Students; and 19. Improvement of Cattle. — Ed.

To this end special organizing bodies or committees should be formed where there are none, and those already in existence should be reformed where necessary. The Kisans are for the most part illiterate. But adults and young persons of school-going age should be educated. This applies to men and women. When they are landless labourers their wages should be brought to a level that would ensure a decent living which should mean balanced food, dwelling houses and clothing, which should satisfy health requirements. Land laws should be investigated. Peasant indebtedness offers a limitless field for research.

2

LABOUR

Closely allied to the Kisan work is 'labour'. Here labour means industrial labour and therefore, concentrated and centralized and much more limited in scope. Moreover, it lends itself readily to political handling.

Being necessarily confined to cities it attracts workers more easily than Kisan work. As part of constructive programme its primary aim is elevation of labour to its deserved status. Therefore a labour worker's aim should be to raise the moral and intellectual height of labour and thus by sheer merit to make him or her capable not merely of bettering his or her material condition but making labour master of the means of production instead of being the slave that it is. Capital should be labour's servant, not its master. Labour should be made conscious of its duty from whose performance rights follow as a matter of course. In a concrete form :

(a) Labour should have its own unions.

(b) Education both general and scientific, of both men and women, should be regularly undertaken through night schools.

(c) Children of labourers should be educated after the basic education style.

(d) There should be a hospital, a creche and a maternity home attached to every centre.

(e) Labour should be able to support itself during strikes. (Labour should be taught the science of conducting a successful non-violent strike.)

All the work I have mentioned could be done only through unions mentioned in (a). To my knowledge the Ahmedabad Union is the best managed union. This does not mean that it has reached my ideal. It is trying to. If all the unions worked in the same direction, the lot of labour would be infinitely better than it is today. Labour united and morally and intellectually trained would any day be superior to capital.

The Hindustan Standard, 28-10-'44

3

VILLAGE WORK

The centre of the village worker's life will be the spinning wheel. The idea at the back of Khadi is that it is an industry supplementary to agriculture and co-extensive with it. The spinning wheel cannot be said to have been established in its own proper place in our life, until we can banish idleness from our villages and make every village home a busy hive.

The worker will not only be spinning regularly but will be working for his bread with the adze or the spade or the last, as the case may be. All his hours minus the eight hours of sleep and rest will be fully occupied with some work. He will have no time to waste. He will allow himself no laziness and allow others none. His life will be a constant lesson to his neighbours in ceaseless and joy-giving industry. Our compulsory or voluntary idleness has to go. If it does not go, no panacea will be of any avail, and semi-starvation will remain the eternal problem that it is. He who eats two grains must produce four. Unless the law is accepted as universal, no amount of reduction in population would serve to solve the problem. If the law is accepted and observed, we have room enough to accommodate millions more to come.

The village worker will thus be a living embodiment of industry. He will master all the processes of Khadi, from cotton-sowing and picking to weaving, and will devote all his thought to perfecting them. If he treats it as a science, it would not jar on him, but he will derive fresh joy from it everyday, as he realizes more and more its great possibilities. If he will go to the village as a teacher, he will go there no less as a learner. He will soon find that he has much to learn from the simple villagers. He will enter into every detail of village life, he will discover the village handicrafts and investigate the possibilities of their growth and their improvement. He may find the villagers completely apathetic to the message of Khadi, but he will, by his life of service, compel interest and attention. Of course, he will not forget his limitations and will not engage, in, for him, the futile task of solving the problem of agricultural indebtedness.

Sanitation and hygiene will engage a good part of his attention. His home and his surroundings will not only be a model of cleanliness, but he will help to promote sanitation in the whole village by taking the broom and the basket round.

He will not attempt to set up a village dispensary or to become the village doctor. These are traps which must be avoided. I happened during my Harijan tour to come across a village where one of our workers who should have known better had built a pretentious building in which he had housed a dispensary and was distributing free medicine to the villages around. In fact, the medicines were being taken from home to home by volunteers and the dispensary was described as boasting a register of 1,200 patients a month ! I had naturally to criticize this severely. That was not the way to do village work, I told him. His duty was to inculcate lessons of hygiene and sanitation in the village folk and thus to show them the way of preventing illness, rather than attempt to cure them. I asked him to leave the palace-like building and to hire it out to the Local Board and to settle in thatched huts. All that one need stock in the way of drugs is quinine, castor oil and iodine and the like. The worker should concentrate more on helping people realize the value of personal and village cleanliness and maintaining it at all cost.

Then he will interest himself in the welfare of the village Harijans. His home will be open to them. In fact, they will turn to him naturally for help in their troubles and difficulties. If the village folk will not suffer him to have the Harijan friends in his house situated in their midst, he must take up his residence in the Harijan quarters.

A word about the knowledge of the alphabet. It has its place, but I should warn you against a misplaced emphasis on it. Do not proceed on the assumption that you cannot proceed with rural instruction without first teaching the children or adults how to read and write. Lots of useful information on current affairs, history, geography and elementary arithmetic, can be given by word of mouth before the alphabet is touched. The eyes, the ears and the tongue come before the hand. Reading comes before writing, and drawing before tracing the letters of the alphabet. If this natural method is followed, the understanding of the children will have a much better opportunity of development than when it is under check by beginning the children's training with the alphabet.

The worker's life will be in tune with the village life. He will not pose as a litterateur buried in his books, loath to listen to details of humdrum life. On the contrary, the people whenever they see him, will find him busy with his tools — spinning wheel, loom, adze, spade, etc. — and always responsive to their meanest inquiries. He will always insist on working for his bread. God has given to everyone the capacity of producing more than his daily needs and, if he will only use his resourcefulness, he will not be in want of an occupation suited to his capacities, however poor they may be. It is more likely than not that the people will gladly maintain him, but it is not improbable that in some places he may be given a cold shoulder. He will still plod on. It is likely that in some villages he may be boycotted for his pro-Harijan proclivities. Let him in that case approach the Harijans and look to them to provide him with food. The labourer is always worthy of his hire and, if he conscientiously serves them, let him not hesitate to accept his food from the Harijans, always provided that he gives more than he takes. In the very early stages, of course, he will draw his meagre allowance from a central fund where such is possible.

Remember that our weapons are spiritual. It is a force that works irresistibly, if imperceptibly. Its progress is geometrical rather than arithmetical. It never ceases so long as there is a propeller behind. The background of all your activities has, therefore, to be spiritual. Hence the necessity for the strictest purity of conduct and character.

You will not tell me that this is an impossible programme, that you have not the qualifications for it. That you have not fulfilled it so far should be no impediment in your way. If it appeals to your reason and your heart, you must not hesitate. Do not fight shy of the experiment. The experiment will itself provide the momentum for more and more effort.

From a talk to workers of the Gujarat Vidyapith

***Harijan*, 31-8-'34**

An ideal Indian village will be so constructed as to lend itself to perfect sanitation. It will have cottages with sufficient light and ventilation built of a material obtainable within a radius of five miles of it. The cottages will have courtyards enabling householders to plant vegetables for domestic use and to house their cattle. The village lanes and streets will be free of all avoidable dust. It will have wells according to its needs and accessible to all. It will have houses of worship for all, also a common meeting place, a village common for grazing its cattle, a co-operative dairy, primary and secondary schools in which industrial education will be the central fact, and it will have Panchayats for settling disputes. It will produce its own grains, vegetables and fruit, and its own Khadi. This is roughly my idea of a model village. In the present circumstances its cottages will remain what they are with slight improvements. Given a good zamindar, where there is one, or co-operation among the people, almost the whole of the programme other than model cottages can be worked out at an expenditure within the means of the villagers including the zamindar or zamindars, without Government assistance. With that assistance there is no limit to the possibility of village reconstruction. But my task just now is to discover what the villagers can do to help themselves if they have mutual co-operation and contribute voluntary labour for the common good. I am convinced that they can, under intelligent guidance, double the village income as distinguished from individual income. There are in our villages inexhaustible resources not for commercial purposes in every case but certainly for local purposes in almost every case. The greatest tragedy is the hopeless unwillingness of the villagers to better their lot.

The very first problem the village worker will solve is its sanitation. It is the most neglected of all the problems that baffle workers and that undermine physical wellbeing and breed disease. If the worker became a voluntary Bhangi, he would begin by collecting night-soil and turning it into manure and sweeping village streets. He will tell people how and where they should perform daily functions and speak to them on the value of sanitation and the great injury caused by its neglect. The worker will continue to do the work whether the villagers listen to him or no.

Harijan, 9-1-'37

If rural reconstruction were not to include rural sanitation, our villages would remain the muck-heaps that they are today. Village sanitation is a vital part of village life and is as difficult as it is important. It needs a heroic effort to eradicate age-long insanitation. The village worker who is ignorant of the science of village sanitation, who is not a successful scavenger, cannot fit himself for village service.

It seems to be generally admitted that without the new or basic education the education of millions of children in India is wellnigh impossible. The village worker has, therefore, to master it, and become a basic education teacher himself.

Adult education will follow in the wake of basic education as a matter of course. Where this new education has taken root, the children themselves become their parents' teachers. Be that as it may, the village worker has to undertake adult education also.

Woman is described as man's better half. As long as she has not the same rights in law as man, as long as the birth of a girl does not receive the same welcome as that of a boy, so long we should know that India is suffering from partial paralysis. Suppression of woman is a denial of Ahimsa. Every village worker will, therefore, regard every woman as his mother, sister or daughter as the case may be, and look upon her with respect. Only such a worker will command the confidence of the village people.

It is impossible for an unhealthy people to win Swaraj. Therefore we should no longer be guilty of the neglect of the health of our people. Every village worker must have a knowledge of the general principles of health.

Without a common language no nation can come into being. Instead of worrying himself with the controversy about Hindi-Hindustani and Urdu, the village worker will acquire a knowledge of the Rashtrabhasha, which should be such as can be understood by both Hindus and Muslims.

Our infatuation for English has made us unfaithful to provincial languages. If only as penance for this unfaithfulness the village worker should cultivate in the villagers a love of their own speech. He will have equal regard for all the other languages of India, and will learn the language of the part where he may be working, and thus be able to inspire the villagers there with a regard for their own speech.

The whole of this programme will, however, be a structure on sand if it is not built on the solid foundation of economic equality. Economic equality must never be supposed to mean possession of an equal amount of worldly goods by everyone. It does mean, however, that everyone will have a proper house to live in, sufficient and balanced food to eat, and sufficient Khadi with which to cover himself. It also means that the cruel inequality that obtains today will be removed by purely non-violent means.

Harijan, 18-8-'40

THE GOAL FOR THE VILLAGE

My idea of Village Swaraj is that it is a complete republic, independent of its neighbours for its vital wants, and yet interdependent for many others in which dependence is a necessity. Thus every village's first concern will be to grow its own food crops and cotton for its cloth. It should have a reserve for its cattle, recreation and playground for adults and children. Then if there is more land available, it will grow *useful* money crops, thus excluding Ganja, tobacco, opium and the like. The village will maintain a village theatre, school and public hall. It will have its own waterworks ensuring clean supply. This can be done through controlled wells and tanks. Education will be compulsory up to the final basic course. As far as possible every activity will be conducted on the co-operative basis. There will be no caste such as we have today with their graded untouchability. Non-violence with its technique of Satyagraha and non-co-operation will be the sanction of the village community. There will be a compulsory service of village guards who will be selected by rotation from the register maintained by the village. The Government of the village will be conducted by the Panchayat of five persons, annually elected by the adult villagers, male and female, possessing minimum prescribed qualifications. These will have all the authority and jurisdiction required. Since there will be no system of punishments in the accepted sense, this Panchayat will be the legislature, judiciary and executive combined to operate for its year of office. Any village can become such a republic today without much interference, even from the present Government whose sole effective connection with the villages is the exaction of the village revenue. I have not examined here the question of relations with the neighbouring villages and the centre if any. My purpose is to present an outline of village government. Here there is perfect democracy based upon individual freedom. The individual is the architect of his own government. The law of non-violence rules him and his government. He and his village are able to defy the might of a world. For the law governing every villager is that he will suffer death in the defence of his and his village's honour.

Harijan, 26-7-'42

4

KHADI AND SPINNING

Khadi connotes the beginning of economic freedom and equality of all in the country. It must be taken with all its implications. It means a wholesale Swadeshi mentality, a determination to find all the necessaries of life in India and that too through the labour and intellect of the villagers. The latter will be largely self-contained and will voluntarily serve the cities of India and even the outside world in so far as it benefits both the parties.

This needs a revolutionary change in the mentality and tastes of many. Easy though the non-violent way is in many respects, it is very difficult in many others. It vitally touches the life of every single Indian, makes him feel aglow with the possession of a power that has lain hidden within himself, and makes him proud of his identity with every drop of the ocean of Indian humanity.

Khadi to me is the symbol of unity of Indian humanity, of its economic freedom and equality and, therefore, ultimately in the poetic expression of Jawaharlal Nehru, 'the livery of India's freedom'.

Moreover, Khadi mentality means decentralization of the production and distribution of the necessaries of life. Therefore, the formula so far evolved is, every village to produce all its necessaries and a certain percentage in addition for the requirements of the cities.

Having explained the implications of Khadi, I must indicate what Congressmen can and should do towards its promotion. Production of Khadi includes cotton growing, picking, ginning, cleaning, carding, slivering, spinning, sizing, dyeing, preparing the warp and the woof, weaving, and washing. These, with the exception of dyeing, are essential processes. Every one of them can be effectively handled in the villages and is being so handled in many villages throughout India which the A. I. S. A. is covering.

If Congressmen will be true to their Congress call in respect of Khadi, they will carry out the instructions of the A. I. S. A. issued from time to time as to the part they can play in Khadi planning. Only a few broad rules can be laid down here :

1. Every family with a plot of ground can grow cotton at least for family use. Cotton growing is an easy process. In Bihar the cultivators were by law compelled to grow indigo on 3/20 of their cultivable land. This was in the interest of the foreign indigo planter. Why cannot we grow cotton voluntarily for the nation on a certain portion of our land ? The reader will note that decentralization commences from the beginning of the Khadi processes. Today cotton crop is centralized and has to be sent to distant parts of India. Before the war it used to be sent principally to Britain and Japan. It was and still is a money crop and, therefore, subject to the fluctuations of the market. Under the Khadi scheme cotton growing becomes free from this uncertainty and gamble. The grower grows what he needs. The farmer needs to know that his first business is to grow for his own needs. When he does that, he will reduce the chance of a low market ruining him.

2. Every spinner would buy — if he has not his own — enough cotton for ginning, which he can easily do without the hand-ginning roller frame. He can gin his own portion with a board and an iron rolling pin. Where this is considered impracticable, hand-ginned cotton should be bought and carded. Carding for self can be done well on a tiny bow without much effort. The greater the

decentralization of labour, the simpler and cheaper the tools. The slivers made, the process of spinning commences.

Imagine the unifying and educative effect of the whole nation simultaneously taking part in the processes up to spinning! Consider the levelling effect of the bond of common labour between the rich and the poor!

If Congressmen will put their heart into the work, they will make improvements in the tools and make many discoveries. In our country there has been a divorce between labour and intelligence. The result has been stagnation. If there is an indissoluble marriage between the two, and that in the manner here suggested, the resultant good will be inestimable.

In this scheme of nation-wide spinning as a sacrifice, I do not expect the average man or woman to give more than one hour daily to this work.

Constructive Programme, 1945; pp. 11-14

THE MESSAGE OF THE SPINNING WHEEL

The message of the spinning wheel is much wider than its circumference. Its message is one of simplicity, service of mankind, living so as not to hurt others, creating an indissoluble bond between the rich and the poor, capital and labour, the prince and the peasant.

Young India, 17-9-'25

I stand by what is implied in the phrase, 'unto this last'. We must do even unto this last as we would have the world do by us. All must have equal opportunity. Given the opportunity, every human being has the same possibility for spiritual growth. That is what the spinning wheel symbolizes.

Harijan, 17-11-'46

SACRIFICIAL SPINNING

'Why should I, who have no need to work for food, spin?' may be the question asked. Because I am eating what does not belong to me. I am living on the spoliation of my countrymen. Trace the course of every pice that finds its way into your pocket, and you will realize the truth of what I write.

I must refuse to insult the naked by giving them clothes they do not need, instead of giving them work which they sorely need. I will not commit the sin of becoming their patron, but on learning that I had assisted in impoverishing them, I would give them neither crumbs nor cast off clothing, but the best of my food and clothes and associate myself with them in work.

God created man to work for his food and said that those who ate without work were thieves.

Young India, 13-10-'21

Service is not possible unless it is rooted in love or Ahimsa. True love is boundless like the ocean and, rising and swelling within one, spreads itself out and crossing all boundaries and frontiers envelops the whole world. This service is again impossible without bread labour, otherwise described in the Gita as Yajna. It is only when a man or woman has done body labour for the sake of service that he or she has a right to live.

Young India, 20-9-'28

I can only think of spinning as the fittest and most acceptable sacrificial body labour. I cannot imagine anything nobler or more national than that for, say one hour in the day, we should all do the labour that the poor must do, and thus identify ourselves with them and through them with all mankind. I cannot imagine better worship of God than that in His name I should labour for the poor even as they do. The spinning wheel spells a more equitable distribution of the riches of the earth.

Young India, 20-10-'21

I ask you to render a slight return to the poor by doing a little Yajna for them. For he who eats without doing his Yajna steals his food, says the Gita. The Yajna of our age and for us is the spinning wheel. Day in and day out I have been talking about it, writing about it.

Young India, 20-1-'27

PLACE OF SPINNING IN VILLAGE ECONOMY

When once we have revived the one industry (Khadi), all the other industries will follow. I would make the spinning wheel the foundation on which to build a sound village life; I would make the wheel the centre round which all other activities will revolve.

Young India, 21-5-'25

The Charkha is a useful and indispensable article for every home. It is the symbol of the nation's prosperity and therefore freedom. It is a symbol not of commercial war but of commercial peace. It bears not a message of ill-will towards the nations of the earth but of goodwill and self-help. It will not need a navy threatening a world's peace and exploiting its resources; but it needs the religious determination of millions to spin their yarn in their own homes as today they cook their food in their own homes.

Young India, 8-12-'21

Hand-spinning does not, it is not intended that it should, compete with, in order to displace, any existing type of industry; it does not aim at withdrawing a single able-bodied person, who can otherwise find a remunerative occupation from his work. The sole claim advanced on its behalf is that it alone offers an immediate, practicable, and permanent solution of that problem of problems that confronts India, viz. the enforced idleness for nearly six months in the year of an overwhelming majority of India's population, owing to lack of a suitable supplementary occupation to agriculture and the chronic starvation of the masses that results therefrom.

Young India, 21-10-26

A starving man thinks first of satisfying his hunger before anything else. He will sell his liberty and all for the sake of getting a morsel of food. Such is the position of millions of the people of India. For them, liberty, God and all such words are merely letters put together without the slightest meaning. They jar upon them. If we want to give these people a sense of freedom we shall have to provide them with work which they can easily do in their desolate homes and which would give them at least the barest living. This can only be done by the spinning wheel. And when they have become self-reliant and are able to support themselves, we are in a position to talk to them about freedom, about Congress etc. Those, therefore, who bring them work and means of getting a crust of bread will be their deliverers and will be also the people who will make them hunger for liberty. Hence the political value of the spinning wheel.

Young India, 18-3-'26

It would necessitate the closest contact of workers with the masses and thus make them one with the people. If successful, it would result in total elimination of foreign cloth, thus reducing, if not altogether destroying, the poisonous influence of foreign capital upon the system of Government prevailing in India. This is its very important political result.

Young India, 5-5-'27

The ideal of Khadi has always been as a means, *par excellence*, for the resuscitation of villages and therethrough the generation of real strength among the masses — the strength that will *ipso facto* bring Swaraj.

Swaraj through Charkha, Compiled by Kanu Gandhi, 1945; p. 8

My experience tells me that in order to make Khadi universal both in the cities and villages, it should be made available only in exchange for yarn. As time passes I hope people will themselves insist on buying Khadi through yarn currency. If, however, this does not happen and they produce yarn grudgingly, I fear Swaraj through non-violence will be impossible.

An increase in the number of mills and cities will certainly not contribute to the prosperity of India's millions. On the contrary, it will bring further poverty to the unemployed and all the diseases that follow in the wake of starvation. If town-dwellers can look upon such a spectacle with equanimity there is nothing more to be said. In such an event it will be the reign of violence in India, not a reign of Truth and Ahimsa. And we shall be forced to admit that there is naturally no room there for Khadi. Military training will then have to be compulsory for all. But we must only think in terms of the starving crores. If they are to be restored, if they are to live, then the Charkha must be made the central activity and people must spin voluntarily.

Swaraj through Charkha, 1945; p. 5

5

EDUCATION AND CULTURE

EDUCATION

Non-violent resistance is the noblest and the best education. It should come, not after the ordinary education in letters of children, but it should precede it. It will not be denied that a child, before it begins to write its alphabet and to gain worldly knowledge, should know what the soul is, what truth is, what love is, what powers are latent in the soul. It should be an essential of real education that a child should learn that, in the struggle of life, it can easily conquer hate by love, untruth by truth, violence by self-suffering. It was because I felt the force of this truth that, during the latter part of the struggle, I endeavoured as much as I could to train the children at Tolstoy Farm and then at Phoenix along these lines.

Speeches and Writings of Mahatma Gandhi, 4th Ed.; p. 189

I hold that true education of the intellect can only come through a proper exercise and training of the bodily organs, e. g. hands, feet, eyes, ears, nose, etc. In other words an intelligent use of the bodily organs in a child provides the best and quickest way of developing his intellect. But unless the development of the mind and body goes hand in hand with a corresponding awakening of the soul, the former alone would prove to be a poor lopsided affair. By spiritual training I mean education of the heart. A proper and all-round development of the mind, therefore, can take place only when it proceeds *pari passu* with the education of the physical and spiritual faculties of the child. They constitute an indivisible whole. According to this theory, therefore, it would be a gross fallacy to suppose that they can be developed piecemeal or independently of one another.

Harijan, 8-5-'37

By education I mean an all-round drawing out of the best in child and man — body, mind and spirit. Literacy is not the end of education nor even the beginning. It is only one of the means whereby man and woman can be educated. Literacy in itself is no education. I would therefore begin the child's education by teaching it a useful handicraft and enabling it to produce from the moment it begins its training.

I hold that the highest development of the mind and the soul is possible under such a system of education. Only every handicraft has to be taught not merely mechanically as is done today but scientifically, i.e. the child should know the why and the wherefore of every process.

Harijan, 31-7-'37

I want that the whole education should be imparted through some handicraft or industry.

You should bear in mind that this primary education would include the elementary principles of sanitation, hygiene, nutrition, of doing their own work, helping parents at home etc. The present generation of boys know no cleanliness, no self-help, and are physically weak. I would therefore, give compulsory physical training through musical drill.

Harijan, 30-10-'37

My plan to impart primary education through the medium of village handicrafts like spinning and carding, etc. is thus conceived as the spearhead of a silent social revolution fraught with the most far-reaching consequences. It will provide a healthy and moral basis of relationship between the city and the village and thus go a long way towards eradicating some of the worst evils of the present social insecurity and poisoned relationship between the classes. It will check the progressive decay of our villages and lay the foundation of a juster social order in which there is no unnatural division between the 'haves' and the 'have-nots' and everybody is assured of a living wage and the right to freedom. And all this would be accomplished without the horror of a bloody class war or a colossal capital expenditure such as would be involved in the mechanization of a vast continent like India. Nor would it entail a helpless dependence on foreign imported machinery or technical skill. Lastly, by obviating the necessity for highly specialized talent, it would place the destiny of the masses, as it were, in their own hands.

Harijan, 9-10-'37

GOAL IN EDUCATION

Q. What is your goal in education when India obtains self-rule?

A. Character-building. I would try to develop courage, strength, virtue, the ability to forget oneself in working towards great aims. This is more important than literacy; academic learning is only a means to this greater end.

Q. Would you try to bring about any specific kind of social organization through education?

A. I would feel that if we succeed in building the character of the individual, society will take care of itself. I would be quite willing to trust the organization of society to individuals so developed.

Remakers of Mankind, By Carlton Washburne, 1932; pp. 104-05

KNOWLEDGE OF OTHER CULTURES

I want the nation to have the treasures contained in that language (English) and for that matter in the other languages of the world, through its own vernaculars. I do not need to learn Bengali in order to know the beauties of Rabindranath's matchless productions. I get them through good translations. Gujarati boys and girls do not need to learn Russian to appreciate Tolstoy's short stories. They learn them through good translations. It is the boast of Englishmen that the best of the world's literary output is in the hands of that nation in simple English inside of a week of its publication. Why need I learn English to get at the best of what Shakespeare and Milton thought and wrote?

It would be good economy to set apart a class of students whose business would be to learn the best of what is to be learnt in the different languages of the world and give the translation in the vernaculars.

Harijan, 9-7-'38

CULTURAL DEVELOPMENT

Nothing can be farther from my thought than that we should become exclusive or erect barriers. But I do respectfully contend that an appreciation of other cultures can fitly follow, never precede, an appreciation and assimilation of our own. It is my firm opinion that no culture has treasures so rich as ours has. We have not known it, we have been made even to deprecate its study and depreciate its value. We have almost ceased to live it. An academic grasp without practice behind it is like an embalmed corpse, perhaps lovely to look at but nothing to inspire or ennoble. My religion forbids me to belittle or disregard other cultures, as it insists under pain of civil suicide upon imbibing and living my own.

Young India, 1-9-'21

THE FUTURE CULTURE OF INDIA

No culture can live, if it attempts to be exclusive. There is no such thing as pure Aryan culture in existence today in India. Whether the Aryans were indigenous to India or were unwelcome intruders, does not interest me much. What does interest me is the fact that my remote ancestors blended with one another with the utmost freedom and we of the present generation are a result of that blend.

Harijan, 9-5-'36

I do not want my house to be walled in on all sides and my windows to be stuffed. I want the cultures of all lands to be blown about my house as freely as possible. But I refuse to be blown off my feet by any. I would have our young men and women with literary tastes to learn as much of English and other world languages as they like, and then expect them to give the benefits of their learning to India and to the world like a Bose, a Roy or the Poet himself. But I would not have a single Indian to forget, neglect or be ashamed of his mother tongue, or to feel that he or she cannot think or express the best thoughts in his or her own vernacular. Mine is not a religion of the prison-house.

Young India, 1-6-'21

It stands for synthesis of the different cultures that have come to stay in India, that have influenced Indian life, and that, in their turn, have themselves been influenced by the spirit of the soil. This synthesis will naturally be of the Swadeshi type, where each culture is assured its legitimate place, and not of the American pattern, where one dominant culture absorbs the rest, and where the aim is not towards harmony, but towards an artificial and forced unity.

Young India, 17-11-'20

6

HEALTH AND HYGIENE

TREATMENT OF DISEASE

Simplicity is the essence of universality. Nothing that is meant for the benefit of the millions requires much erudition. The latter can be acquired only by the few and therefore can benefit the rich only. But India lives in her seven lakhs of villages — obscure, tiny, out-of-the-way villages, where the population in some cases hardly exceeds a few hundred, very often not even a few score. That is real India, my India, for which I live. You cannot take to these humble people the paraphernalia of highly qualified doctors and hospital equipment. In simple natural remedies and Ramanama lies their only hope.

Harijan, 7-4-'46

I hold that where the rules of personal, domestic and public sanitation are strictly observed and due care is taken in the matter of diet and exercise, there should be no occasion for illness or disease. Where there is absolute purity, inner and outer, illness becomes impossible.

Harijan, 26-5-'46

And, while obeying all the laws of nature in order to cure illness, if it does come, the sovereign remedy ever lies in Ramanama. But this cure through Ramanama cannot become universal in the twinkling of an eye. To carry conviction to the patient, the physician has to be a living embodiment of the power of Ramanama. Meantime, all that can possibly be had from the five agents of nature must be taken and used. They are earth, water, ether, fire and wind. This, to my mind, is the limit of nature cure. Therefore, my experiment in Uruli Kanchan consists in teaching the villagers how to live clean and healthy lives and in trying to cure the sick through the proper use of the five agents. If necessary, curative herbs that grow locally, may be used. Wholesome and balanced diet is, of course, an indispensable part of nature cure.

***Harijan*, 11-8-'46**

7

THE DRINK AND DRUG EVIL

Those unfortunate men who have become slaves to the habit, require to be helped against themselves. Some of them even ask to be helped. You will not be deceived by the specious argument that India must not be made sober by compulsion and that those who wish to drink must have facilities provided for them. The State does not cater for the vices of its people. We do not regulate or license houses of ill-fame. We do not provide facilities for thieves to indulge their propensity for thieving. I hold drink to be more damnable than thieving and perhaps even prostitution. Is it not often the parent of both ? I ask you to join the country in sweeping out of existence the drink revenue and abolishing the liquor-shops.

Young India, 8-6-'21

Drinks and drugs degrade those who are addicted to them and those who traffic in them. The drunkard forgets the distinction between wife, mother and sister and indulges in crimes of which in his sober moments he will be ashamed. Any one who has anything to do with labour knows to what state the labourers are reduced when they are under the satanic influence of drink. Nor are the other classes better of. I have known the captain of a ship forgetting himself in his drunken state. The ship had to be entrusted to the care of the chief officer. Barristers having drunk have been known to be rolling in gutters.

Young India, 4-2-'26

Drugs and drink are the two arms of the devil with which he strikes his helpless slaves into stupefaction and intoxication.

Young India, 22-4-'26

I hold drinking spirituous liquors in India to be more criminal than the petty thefts which I see starving men and women committing and for which they are prosecuted and punished. I do tolerate, very unwillingly it is true and helplessly, because of want of full realization of the law of love, a moderate system of penal code. And so long as I do, I must advocate the summary punishment of those who manufacture the fiery liquid and those even who will persist in drinking it notwithstanding repeated warnings. I do not hesitate forcibly to prevent my children from rushing into fire or deep waters. Rushing to red water is far more dangerous than rushing to a raging furnace or flooded stream. The latter destroys only the body, the former destroys both body and soul.

Young India, 8-8-'29

If I was appointed dictator for one hour for all India, the first thing I would do would be to close without compensation all the liquor shops, and compel factory owners to produce humane conditions for their workmen and open refreshment and recreation rooms where these workmen would get innocent drinks and equally innocent amusements.

Young India, 25-6-'31

NEED FOR PRIVATE EFFORT

The work in connection with the liquor habit has got to be primarily done by us. The utmost that the Government can do or be made to do in this respect is to cease issuing toddy licences but it can hardly wean the drunkard from his evil habit. That part of the work will still have to be undertaken by private effort.

Young India, 13-9-'28

If we are to reach our goal through non-violent effort, we may not leave to the future Government the fate of lakhs of men and women who are labouring under the curse of intoxicants and narcotics.

Medical men can make a most effective contribution towards the removal of this evil. They have to discover ways of weaning the drunkard and the opium-addict from the curse.

Women and students have a special opportunity in advancing this reform. By many acts of loving service they can acquire on addicts a hold which will compel them to listen to the appeal to give up the evil habit.

Congress Committees can open recreation booths where the tired labourer will rest his limbs, get healthy and cheap refreshments, and find suitable games. All this work is fascinating and uplifting. The non-violent approach to Swaraj is a novel approach. In it, old values give place to new. In the violent way such reforms may find no place. Believers in that way, in their impatience and, shall I say, ignorance, put off such things to the day of deliverance. They forget that lasting and healthy deliverance comes from within, i.e. from self-purification. Constructive workers make legal prohibition easy and successful even if they do not pave the way for it.

Constructive Programme, 1941; pp. 10, 11

GAMBLING

The Sardar and his volunteers poured into my ears harrowing tales of the havoc that gambling was working in the villages of Gujarat. It is spreading like grass fire of a windy night. Everybody is in a hurry to be rich without working. 'Somebody will have made the correct guess as to the ruling price for the day of some commodity. Why not I?' argues the gambler and rushes to his ruin. Peace is being destroyed in the once happy homes of Gujarat.

There is no doubt that whatever one calls it, this gambling is as old as Adam, and that though the form and the name may have changed, the substance has not changed at all.

The law must be against this gambling. But it is of no avail if public opinion is not behind it. It is therefore necessary for workers to bestir themselves as they did during the plague or as they have done for the earthquake relief. They must not be satisfied till the evil is rooted out. In a way it is worse than the plague or the quake. For it destroys the soul within. A person without the soul is a burden upon the earth. No doubt war against gambling is not so simple as war against plague or earthquake distress. In the latter there is more or less co-operation from the sufferers. In the former the sufferers invite and hug their sufferings. To wean the gambler from his vice is like weaning the drunkard from the drink habit. This war against gambling is therefore an uphill task. But it must be tackled.

Harijan, 15-6-'35

I know nothing of horse-racing. I have ever looked upon it with horror for its associations. I know that many men have been ruined on the race-course.

Young India, 27-4-'21

Gambling on the race-course is, so far as I am aware, an importation like many other importations, from the West, and if I had my way I would withdraw the protection of the law that gambling on the race-course enjoys even to the extent it does. I have heard it argued that horse-racing is necessary for breeding good horses. There may be truth in this. Is it not possible to have horse-racing without gambling, or is gambling also an aid to the good breeding of horses ?

Harijan, 4-9-'37

8

WOMEN

Woman has been suppressed under custom and law for which man was responsible and in the shaping of which she had no hand. In a plan of life based on non-violence, woman has as much right to shape her own destiny as man has to shape his. But as every right in a non-violent society proceeds from the previous performance of a duty, it follows that rules of social conduct must be framed by mutual co-operation and consultation. They can never be imposed from outside. Men have not realized this truth in its fulness in their behaviour towards women. They have considered themselves to be lords and masters of women instead of considering them as their friends and co-workers. It is the privilege of Congressmen to give the women of India a lifting hand. Women are in the position somewhat of the slave of old who did not know that he could or ever had to be free. And when freedom came, for the moment he felt helpless. Women have been taught to regard themselves as slaves of men. It is up to Congressmen to see that they enable them to realize their full status and play their part as equals of men.

This revolution is easy, if the mind is made up. Let Congressmen begin with their own homes. Wives should not be dolls and objects of indulgence, but should be treated as honoured comrades in common service. To this end those who have not received a liberal education should receive such instruction as is possible from their husbands. The same observation applies, with the necessary changes, to mothers and daughters.

It is hardly necessary to point out that I have given a one-sided picture of the helpless state of India's women. I am quite conscious of the fact that in the villages generally they hold their own with their men folk and in some respects even rule them. But to the impartial outsider the legal and customary status of woman is bad enough throughout and demands radical alteration.

Constructive Programme, 1941; pp. 17, 18

9

COMMUNAL UNITY

Everybody is agreed about the necessity of this unity. But everybody does not know that unity does not mean political unity which may be imposed. It means an unbreakable heart unity. The first thing essential for achieving such unity is for every Congressman, whatever his religion may be, to represent in his own person Hindu, Muslim, Christian, Zoroastrian, Jew etc., shortly, every Hindu and non-Hindu. He has to feel his identity with every one of the millions of the inhabitants of Hindustan. In order to realize this, every Congressman will cultivate personal friendship with persons representing faiths other than his own. He should have the same regard for the other faiths as he has for his own.

Constructive Programme, 1941 ; p. 8

10

REMOVAL OF UNTOUCHABILITY

Untouchability is not only not a part and parcel of Hinduism, but a plague, which it is the bounden duty of every Hindu to combat. Every Hindu, therefore, who considers it a sin, should atone for it by fraternizing with 'untouchables', associating with them in a spirit of love and service, deeming himself purified by such acts, redressing their grievances, helping them patiently to overcome ignorance and other evils due to the slavery of ages, and inspiring other Hindus to do likewise.

From Yeravda Mandir, 1945 ; p. 32

At this time of the day it is unnecessary to dilate upon the necessity of the removal of this blot and curse upon Hinduism. Congressmen have certainly done much in this matter. But I am sorry to have to say that many Congressmen have looked upon this item as a mere political necessity and not something indispensable, so far as Hindus are concerned, for the very existence of Hinduism. If Hindu Congressmen take up the cause for its own sake, they will influence the so-called Sanatanis far more extensively than they have hitherto done. They should approach them not in a militant spirit but, as befits their non-violence, in a spirit of friendliness. And so far as the Harijans are concerned, every Hindu should make common cause with them and befriend them in their awful isolation — such isolation as perhaps the world has never seen in the monstrous immensity one witnesses in India. I know from experience how difficult the task is. But it is part of the task of building the edifice of Swaraj.

Constructive Programme, 1941; pp. 9, 10

11

ECONOMIC EQUALITY

This last is the master key to non-violent independence. Working for economic equality means abolishing the eternal conflict between capital and labour. It means the levelling down of the few rich in whose hands is concentrated the bulk of the nation's wealth on the one hand, and the levelling up of the semi-starved naked millions on the other. A non-violent system of government is clearly an impossibility so long as the wide gulf between the rich and the hungry millions persists.

I adhere to my doctrine of trusteeship in spite of the ridicule that has been poured upon it. It is true that it is difficult to reach. So is non-violence.

This non-violent experiment is still in the making. We have nothing much yet to show by way of demonstration. It is certain, however, that the method has begun to work though ever so slowly in the direction of equality. And since non-violence is a process of conversion, the conversion, if achieved, must be permanent.

It (non-violent Swaraj) will not drop from heaven all of a sudden one fine morning. But it has to be built up brick by brick by corporate self-effort. We have travelled a fair way in that direction. But a much longer and weary distance has to be covered before we can behold Swaraj (Sarvodaya) in its glorious majesty.

Constructive Programme, 1941; pp. 21, 22

Let us consider how equal distribution can be brought about through non-violence. The first step towards it is for him who has made this ideal part of his being to bring about the necessary changes in his personal life. He would reduce his wants to a minimum, bearing in mind the poverty of India. His earnings would be free of dishonesty. The desire for speculation would be renounced. His habitation would be in keeping with his new mode of life. There would be self-restraint exercised in every sphere of life. When he has done all that is possible in his own life, then only will he be in a position to preach this ideal among his associates and neighbours.

Harijan, 25-8-'40

NON-VIOLENCE, THE MEANS

I shall bring about economic equality through non-violence, by converting the people to my point of view by harnessing the forces of love as against hatred. I will not wait till I have converted the whole society to my view but will straightaway make a beginning with myself. It goes without saying that I cannot hope to bring about economic equality of my conception, if I am the owner of fifty motor cars or even of ten Bighas of land. For that I have to reduce myself to the level of the poorest of the poor. That is what I have been trying to do for the last fifty years or more.

Harijan, 31-3-'46

Impure means result in an impure end. Hence the prince and the peasant will not be equalized by cutting off the prince's head, nor can the process of cutting off equalize the employer and the employed. One cannot reach truth by untruthfulness.

Therefore, only truthful, non-violent and pure-hearted Socialists will be able to establish a socialistic society in India and the world.

Harijan, 13-7-'47

CONCLUSION: LET US GO FORWARD

We have not been able yet to discover the true measure of the innumerable properties of an article of daily use like water. Some of its properties fill us with wonder. Let us not, therefore, make light of a force of the subtlest kind of Ahimsa, and let us try to discover its hidden power with patience and faith. Within a brief space of time we have carried to a fairly successful conclusion a great experiment in the use of this force. As you know I have not set much store by it. Indeed I have hesitated even to call it an experiment in Ahimsa. But according to the legend, as Rama's name was enough to float stones, even so the movement carried on in the name of Ahimsa brought about a great awakening in the country and carried us ahead. It is difficult to forecast the possibilities when men with unflinching faith carry this experiment further forward.

Harijan, 28-7-'40

SARVODAYA

PART II

By Vinoba Bhave and others

SECTION EIGHT: THE NEW REVOLUTION

1

THE NEW REVOLUTION

(*By Vinoba*)

People want a revolutionary programme and think that a revolution cannot be wrought without bloodshed. Let me tell you, I cannot accept their contention. Those who think that a revolution cannot be wrought without bloodshed are not revolutionists at all. They are *status quo-ists* (*jaise-the-vadi*). The object before them is not a revolution but bringing about an exchange of places of the present unhappy and happy ones. Is that a revolution? What change has come, except that those who are happy, become unhappy and the unhappy become happy? Have they been able to eliminate misery altogether? It is for this reason that I call it status-quo-ism. A revolution must signify universal happiness without exception. Being a Sarvodayist, who wants to try for universal happiness and nothing less than universal happiness, I claim to be a revolutionist. Those who want to divide society into two classes, may call themselves Communists or any other-ists; but they are all, in my humble opinion, Communalists. While the Western mind is trained to think in terms of the greatest good of the greatest number, the Indian mind, from its very childhood, is taught to think in terms of the good of all. His mind is trained to love all, though he may be able to serve but few. There was a time when a microscopic minority enjoyed at the cost of a great majority. Today, the majority wants to be happy at the cost of the minority. But in India, quite contrary to this we are taught to do unto others as we would like to be done unto ourselves. In the language of the Gita, it is called 'Atmaupamya'. I want to transform the whole society on this basis, and it is for these reasons that my method is a revolutionary one. Does not the bee collect honey without causing any harm to the flowers? I too want to achieve results without causing much hardship to others. This can be realized if we have faith in the principle of change of heart. I am therefore doing nothing new, but carrying out what the sages have taught us. I have not the slightest doubt that if this non-violent revolution is not achieved in India, it cannot be achieved anywhere else.

Harijan, 15-12-'51

Rule of the majority is the law of the day; whether the majority has or has not scruples and character, it does not matter at all. Is not rule of the majority only brute force? How can you differentiate between the rule of the regiment, rule of money and rule of the majority? What is it if it is not brute force?

Harijan, 17-1-'53

The right thing to do for every one, Vinoba said, was to pray to God that he should have strength to exercise his will only upon himself, and never impose it on others. If others approve of his idea, let them take it up by their own free choice. That should be a matter of satisfaction to him, but his prayer should be that he might never impose his will upon others by force, even for the good of those others. So long as people insisted on imposing their ideas on others without any regard to whether these others had understood or accepted them, the seeds of violence, imperialism and world wars would not be rooted out.

Some of them tended to grow impatient at times and said they could not wait until all were trained to do the right thing of their own accord with understanding, that the better and more effective way was to set up an appropriately ordered system and compel people to adapt themselves to it and training would gradually follow. They felt a sense of frustration in labouring at educating, and showed more zeal in piling up arms.

As against this Vinoba pointed out that a system might appear to succeed for some time, but if it lacked foundation in education, dissatisfaction would follow and once again there would arise the demand for a new type of organization. Thus a rapid cycle of organization, disorganization and demand for a new type of organization continued endlessly, because no organization was set up with the intelligent consent of the people.

They, therefore, had to steer clear of the illusion that they could achieve anything merely by substituting a new organization for the old one. On the other hand, they must pin their faith on educating the people and carry on with courage and bide their time patiently till it was achieved. This would be found to be the shortest road to their goal. No one should do anything without fully understanding it, nor should any one feel pleased if people did anything even when it was good, merely out of respect or consideration for him or from a sense of fear or submission to another. Lord Shrikrishna tendered his best advice to Arjuna but at the end asked him to do as he liked (यथेच्छसि तथा कुरु ।) That should be their ideal. There should be no compulsion. Then only could they bring about a society based on Ahimsa, and hope for lasting peace.

Harijan, 7-7-'51

SECTION NINE: ECONOMIC EQUALITY

1

ECONOMIC EQUALITY

(*By Vinoba*)

The services of a scavenger, a mother, a professor, and numerous others of that type cannot be determined in terms of money. Therefore the rule should be: A man who wholeheartedly serves society should be held entitled to his living wage. Likewise, the President of the country, who serves his country with equal zeal, although intellectually, should be given the wage sufficient for his living. The basis of payment to the President must be the same as that to the Kisan and the scavenger. I have served society in various capacities, as professor, judge, peasant, writer, editor etc.; but I never felt that one type of work was of a higher type than that of another. I derived the same mental satisfaction from every one of them. It is however true that I did not get the same experience of muscular exertion from every work. It differed in each type of work. But that does not make any difference in the degree of mental satisfaction. When anybody desires to give me more than I need I feel perplexed. I cannot accept it. Why should I take more curds than what I need? And I am at a loss to know why I should accept it, simply because somebody offers it. The right principle is: Every one must have his bread for the day and not also for the morrow. And the economic, social and spiritual value of every work should be equal. Thus alone can Samya-yoga be established.

I do not say that everyone should get an equal share in the total cultivable land. I do not want arithmetical equality, but I do want equity, or such equality as, for instance, the five fingers of the hand have. These five fingers are not equal in dimensions, but they all work in full co-operation and together perform innumerable tasks.

Again, their inequality is not as disproportionate as it would be if, say, the smallest finger were an inch in length, while the largest one was a foot. The moral is that even if there cannot be absolute equality, there should also not be disproportionate inequality, but there should be equity, even through their inequality. The five fingers possess different powers. Similarly each man possesses a different capacity. All these inherent capacities of each person should be developed. This is called Panchayat Dharma.

From his speech at the U. P. Sarvodaya Conference on 1-11-'51

Harijan, 26-1-'52

2

AN EQUITABLE WAGE

(*By J. C. Kumarappa*)

In capitalistic economics labour is dealt with as a commodity to be bought and sold. So wages appear as a price for this human commodity. It is completely detached of fundamental human considerations. An industrialist buys human labour with the same heart as he buys high-speed steel. Naturally therefore he is out to beat down prices and get the most he can out of the bargain. This is the order of exploitation and cannot be changed as long as human labour is dealt with as a commodity.

Where we desire to deal with man as a human being, the consideration should be based on social values. The price we pay for human labour should be calculated not on the basis of the market price that will be fetched by any commodity to be produced but on what it will cost to maintain the producer. If a palm tapper requires a balanced diet, like any other human being, and he requires also a weather-proof house to live in sanitary and hygienic conditions with enough amenities and facilities to bring up his children in the way that a worthy citizen would be expected to do, then such a standard of living should be worked out for a tapper's family. And this should form an irreducible minimum cost of his labour. Supposing his requirements are equivalent to a present day money income of Rs 150/- per month, then we should calculate how much marketable commodities a conscientious and skilled tapper will produce with his labour in a month and spread that money income of that tapper over the market price of the commodity. One may even imagine, by so doing we may raise the price of Gur to Re. 1-8-0 per seer. But we should not be afraid of high prices if we aim at bringing about social justice. As a matter of fact, when the Government fixes prices and undertakes to sell commodities we shall be eliminating quite a number of middlemen and the intermediate commissions. Once we fix prices in this fashion the Government should cut down various forms of competition such as from capitalists and industrialists and from foreign imports. Actually only by this way we can ever hope to raise the standard of living of our producers.

This need not be ruled out as an impracticable suggestion. Nearly one third of the world living under the inspiration of Russian social justice is based on such considerations in regulating their standard of living through price mechanism.

Gram Udyog Patrika, July '53, p. 41

3

DISCRIMINATIVE EQUALITY

(*By Vinoba*)

Equality does not mean that every one should have five acres of land, and the same kind of house, or an equal yardage of cloth. We only want that the things, which are necessary for life, such as air, water and land, should be equally accessible to all. None will grudge the surplus which may be left over with some after all have had enough of these things.

We want equality tempered with discrimination. The mother does not distribute food among her children on the basis of mathematical equality. To the youngest one she gives only milk, to the next some milk and some bread, and to the grown-ups only bread. In the same way, in society also we will exercise discrimination and take into account the intensity of hunger and the power of digestion of each in the distribution of food. Where equality is brought about by force, all are compelled to conform to the same pattern. We are totally against this kind of regimentation. We aim at spiritual equality based on discrimination.

Harijan, 20-12-'52

4

EQUALITY AND KINDNESS

(*By Vinoba*)

Some people were prone to aver offhand that they were not interested in kindness, which old poets, religions and ancient teachers had eulogized. They wanted equality and not kindness, which bred egoism. But, Vinoba warned, if they wanted to bring about equality along with a decrial of kindness, they deprived themselves of a great spiritual force and created an unnecessary antagonism. They should realize that there was antagonism between equality and inequality, and not between equality and kindness. Their approach to equality, therefore, should be so devised that they might get for its furtherance the benefit of all the moral and spiritual power of those who had developed kindness. It was not necessary to set one's face against kindness; but to regard that through kindness, which they had practised hitherto, they had discovered that real kindness consisted in the establishment of equality. The practice of a little kindness was good in an order of inequality; it gave some consolation to the soul. But it was not enough, and it fell short of true kindness, which could be built only on the establishment of equality. If this approach was adopted, it would enable them to inherit the benefits of the assiduous efforts of their forefathers for the development of kindness, and utilize them for building up the new effort for equality. They should not, therefore, commit the mistake of destroying the old tradition of cultivating kindness and plant the idea of equality as though it were quite new and opposed to the old tradition.

The people of the present age were taking a step forward to realize equality in actual life. In doing so, they should muster on their side the cumulative effort of their forefathers who had meditated on it with great patience. They too should ceaselessly meditate on that ideal. They had commenced a new stage on the path of evolution. It was like beginning a new chapter of a book. Hence they should bestow on it the same careful attention as a writer would do on his book. They knew how kindness could be illusory and gave rise on the one side to vaingloriousness, and on the other, to poverty and pitiful conditions. If they were not watchful, the same might happen to equality and deprive them of the faculty of right discrimination. If equality destroyed the faculty of discrimination, it itself could not last long, and would prove to be an illusion. Again, if equality was brought about at the cost of discrimination, it would be necessary to recover the latter, entailing for the purpose, an effort extending to several centuries more. They, therefore, had to evolve an equality accompanied with right discrimination and partaking of the fully developed kindness. That would require constant self-examination and rejection of all the dross which tended to obscure the mind. Every trace of egoism that made for inequality and the sense of high and low would have to be hunted to its source and driven out. If they set about it humbly and sincerely, they would find to their surprise that each of them had a lot to do to approximate to the ideal. Even he, Vinoba said, who being a non-possessor of private property, might be supposed to have not much to do in the field of equality, so far as economic equality is concerned, would find a lot remaining to be done. A close examination of his mind would reveal that even he had much leeway to make. Then there were inequalities which arose from physical differences. They too would have to be resolved.

There was still another consideration, which was important for the success of an idea. They had to achieve a hundred times more equality in their individual lives than what they wanted to bring about in society. There could be no prospect for success until this was done. The human body was able to maintain a temperature 98 ° F., only because the source of all heat, namely the sun, was hot to an infinite degree. They could well imagine what would happen to their bodies if the sun too were no warmer than the human body, i.e. 98 ° F. The Sevaks therefore owed to themselves to be far ahead of society in this respect. Then only would their noble aspirations and actions be successful.

Harijan, 30-6-'51

5

DIFFERENCE BETWEEN COMMUNISM AND SARVODAYA

(By K. G. Mashruwala)

The difference between Communism and Sarvodaya is not in the ends but in the means. Gandhiji himself more than once declared that he was a Communist *minus* their violence. The latter difference he expressed in positive language by saying that he did not propagate Samyavada (the theory or ideology of Communism) but Samyadharma (the practice or duty of equality). His endeavour till the end of his life was to practise this Dharma. He tried to identify himself with the humblest section of Indians. He was born in a family which for some generations had practised administration and politics as a career. Though he could not escape fulfilling that destiny, he did not take to it as such but went in for the one next to it — namely, law. He read Ruskin, and discovered that even if he practised law, he was not justified in making it a means of amassing wealth for himself. So he deprived himself of all private property. He read Tolstoy and the Gita and came to the conclusion that law was not a 'productive' occupation, and that he must earn his livelihood by producing something by his own physical labour. And so from law he turned to land, and described himself a Kisan. An agriculturist, however, owns some property, and has a superior social and economic status to that of artisans. So he became a weaver. But a weaver is far better off than a land labourer and he, too, far higher than a Bhangi, who has no implements, no technical skill, no knowledge and no status in society. And so Gandhiji called himself a Bhangi, tried to live amongst them, befriend them, and raise the condition of this humble brotherhood of his.

The more he practised equality, the more he realized how difficult it is to live by it. He could not say that he had succeeded in doing so. And so, while he steadily endeavoured to reach that goal as much as he could, he did not find it in his heart to feel angry towards those who took for granted exploitation and inequality in economic and social conditions in the same way as we take for granted the exploitation of the cow and the bullock and the inequality of status between these animals and ourselves. The capitalist idea is imbedded in the poorest citizen of the country. Everyone, if he can, wants some day to be a landholder or a capitalist and to create conditions in which he will not have to work for his daily food — at any rate, not do physical work. It is the aspiration to get an opportunity to lead a comfortable and physically non-laborious life which, on the one hand, reconciles people to inequalities of life and status, and on the other hand, to feel jealous of those who have preceded them in this aspiration. Since none of them believes in simple, hard, laborious life, though one is called a capitalist and the other a Communist, both are but rival claimants for the same Gadi of ease and comfort. As long as man regards comforts and freedom from work as boons of life, he will not escape resorting to violence to achieve his end.

If non-violence and bread labour are accepted as an inseparable part of the Communist movement, there can be no reason for a quarrel with it. Sympathy for Communism must lead us to seek appropriate non-violent methods of bringing about these changes in the social and economic order, which the Communists want to effect through violence.

Harijan, 5-6-'49

SECTION TEN: LABOUR, NOT MONEY, THE BASIS

1

THE DIGNITY OF LABOUR

(*By Vinoba*)

The idea has taken firm root in the minds of people that those who do manual work are inferior beings. Labour has lost its dignity as well as its worth. It was under these conditions that foreigners conquered our country.

Such a state of affairs has to be ended and all those who produce should be regarded as the true citizens of India. They should be honoured by society and should receive decent living wages. Their life should be made so happy that others may feel envious of their lot.

From his speech at Delhi on 18-10-'51
Harijan, 19-1-'52

2

TO THE MIDDLE CLASSES

(*By C. Rajagopalachari*)

There should at once be a determined effort to reduce if not to eliminate the dependence on the labour of others. Simplify life and try to do everything yourselves. Both men and women should follow this unpleasant prescription in domestic life. There may be much inconvenience felt in the change, especially when it is undertaken in right earnest and not as a token. But as the new way of life proceeds, it will unfold joys which before were not known. In the West, the middle classes even now follow this prescription with pride and pleasure. But then they have, and we have not in our country, many labour-saving appliances. We cannot command identical conditions in any matter. We should all the same take lessons and try to apply the principles learnt in spite of the greater difficulty in our own country and its conditions. Labour-saving appliances have again a knack of turning out to be dependence on others in a concentrated form and liable to result in the same breakdown as plain dependence. Let us therefore not pine away, but work for true independence, that is, non-dependence on others in daily life. Neither political independence nor political democracy is enough for true happiness. We have to equalize in all respects. Unless we all work in the physical sense, we cannot stabilize democracy. There should be no distinctions of status in work. All tasks should be deemed equally noble and as forms of piety and homage to the household gods. Otherwise we must submit to be ruled by the people who are prepared to work and our lives have to be on sufference. A new and necessary middle class will arise, not a middle class based on birth but a true middle class of manual workers, those who have attained skill and status by work and learning, who can design, guide and teach, the members of which go down or up according to talent, industry or circumstance, and who do not come to position by birth only.

The present structure of a 'middle' class based on birth must become a thing of the past. It can be achieved voluntarily and this would be preferable. Let us begin by tasks gone through in all schools and colleges under the guidance of teachers who will not allow simulation and snobbery.

Harijan, 9-2-'52

3

NEED FOR PRODUCTIVE LABOUR

(*By Vinoba*)

What is the cause of our problems ? To my mind, it is want of love for manual labour. I do not think that our population, large as it is, is too big to be maintained in the country. If there are many mouths, the hands too are many. But the hands do not labour with love ; they regard work as an infliction instead of as a privilege. So the hands do not produce their utmost but only what they unavoidably must. Everyone claims his full share for the mouth but not in the work to be done by the hands. This want of devotion for work is a greater misfortune even than want of sufficient production.

I regard this as an age-long defect in us. We are never in want of finding an excuse for suspending work. If it is Ramanavami or a day of observance we must have a holiday ; we would also cease work if it is a day of festival, say, Divali, or a marriage in the family, or the birth of a son, or the birthday of Gandhiji. We do not wish to work if there is a death, or anniversary of death of a family member, or again of, say, Gandhiji. If we have a guest in the house, or the arrival of a great leader in the town, it is a sufficient reason for us to suspend work. In short, we would not let go a single excuse if thereby we could have an opportunity to keep our hands idle.

It was not merely for producing Khaddar that Gandhiji laid the greatest stress upon spinning. Of course, spinning would produce Khaddar ; but the stress was on the revolution involved in the insistence on productive work. He placed before the nation a type of physical work which, besides producing wealth, was such as could be done by the aged and the young alike. Productive labour is not a thing from which anyone who can at all work, should claim an exception. All those who take a share in the consumption of goods, must also take a share in their production. A judge or a teacher may not say that he is rendering some other service to society. For, he does not live on books and records alone but also on food, and needs cloth like all other beings. He must therefore share directly in their production.

But unfortunately the Congress could not understand Gandhiji and attached more importance to the payment of four annas than to yarn. It made the usual confusion between wealth and money. It was not realized that payment in the shape of hand-spun yarn was payment through production of new wealth, which the payment in the shape of money was not. Money, we have plenty of, at present; but wealth, which indicates prosperity has diminished. If we give prestige to money, the prestige of labour is necessarily reduced. Under Gandhiji's scheme, a person giving a *lakh* of rupees to the Congress would have been considered its donor but not a member entitled to vote. The contributor of hand-spun *yarn* would have become the voter. It was a revolutionary idea, which the Congress failed to understand.

From a post-prayer speech delivered on 10-3-'49
***Harijan*, 17-4-'49**

4

KHADI, SYMBOLIC OF SELF-RELIANT LABOUR

(*By K. G. Mashruwala*)

Khadi is the centre of Gandhiji's constructive programme not only for India but for the whole world. It must be remembered that Khadi is not confined to cotton fabrics only. Home-spun and home-woven woollen and silk apparel is also Khadi, and on a full consideration of the Sarvodaya ideal it should not be difficult for one to realize that not only in India but in the most mechanized and industrialized countries of Europe and America also, every home must become as self-reliant as possible about this necessity of life. In fact, as Shri Vinoba has pointed out some months ago, in a civilized society the first necessity of man is not so much food as cloth. You can go about anywhere in the world without feeling ashamed even if you have remained hungry for some days. But modern civilized society does not allow you to move about naked even in all the parts of your house, and hence even though it may not be possible for every man to grow his own food, he should produce at least his own cloth; and fortunately this is much simpler and more within one's own power than the production of food. Besides, on the moral plane, Khadi is particularly the emblem of a peaceful and non-violent order. It is suggestive of industriousness, bread labour, non-exploitation and self-expression. I do not know how far this will be realized by admirers of the Sarvodaya movement. But as Shri Kakasaheb Kalelkar boldly prophesied, a day will come when this proposition perhaps will be accepted as obvious, and an Indian going abroad will not hesitate to put the Charkha and the handloom before the most industrialized people of the world.

Harijan, 27-3-'49

5

MANUAL LABOUR

Vinoba is engaged at present in a great experiment at his Ashram at Paramdham, Paunar, for reducing the use of money as far as possible. According to him, money as the sole medium of exchange has done greater mischief and havoc in the world than anything else. He was engrossed, along with his few companions, in the task of adding to the production of the land with the simplest of implements, not depending even on bullocks for tilling the land. He wants to see what the extreme form of manual labour can achieve in agriculture in the present circumstances, where pumps, machines and tractors are considered to be the most up-to-date and scientific implements of agriculture.

The thesis which he propounded at Shivarampalli whenever he found an opportunity to do it was the sacredness of labour and the new orientation of the whole constructive programme through it. The purity derived from simple manual labour and revaluation of all our values in the present civilized world through this value is, according to Acharya Vinoba, the panacea for all our ills and difficulties. If we eliminate money currency and take to labour with a new faith, fervour and piety, the condition of the world would be revolutionized. The need of the hour is production and greater production with this new ideal. Vinoba repeatedly pointed out that if we utilized to the fullest extent our hands with the barest and simplest of instruments at our command, our needs will be more than satisfied. Non-exploitation, decentralized society, simplicity, beauty of life and economic equality will be necessarily achieved if we learn to look at manual labour from this new point of view.

Harijan, 28-4-'51

6

FREEDOM FROM MONEY

(*By Vinoba*)

In his post-prayer speech at Rajghat, Delhi, Vinobaji remarked that village economy should be based on labour, after money was eliminated. Some people imagined he wanted to go back to the old barter system. That was not his plan at all. He was not against currency. Actually, he preferred paper currency to coinage. But the currency he wanted was of labour. It should not be printed at Nasik at the behest of some ruler. It should be a currency adopted by the villagers themselves for their own use. In this currency there should be no question of any credit.

Harijan, 29-12-'51

7

NON-POSSESSION AND INSTITUTIONS

(*By Vinoba*)

Some do not hoard for themselves, but allow themselves to do so for their institutions. It is like a man who will not kill for himself, but will do it in the name of a cause or for his country. In my opinion both possessions are equally bad and lead to inconsistency. For instance, the Charkha Sangh has balances which it deposits in banks. This is done in order to get interest. Obviously it has more funds than it is able to utilize for the cause of the Charkha. But how are banks able to pay interest? They employ the loans in various profitable industries. Now look at the self-contradiction. Being earmarked for Charkha activity the Charkha Sangh cannot invest its funds in Go-Seva, although it is one of the items of the constructive programme accepted by it. But they can be and are invested through the medium of banks in large-scale industries! This contradiction arises on account of our greed for possessing money even though it may be in the name of our institutions. The same is the story of the Kasturba Fund, and it will be the same with the Gandhi Memorial Fund. Why do we need to collect so much money? If that amount is really necessary, it should be possible to spend it in one or two years. But this does not take place and no one sees the wrong involved in getting income by investing these funds in banks. The reason is that we have been brought up in a society in which not to earn interest is regarded as folly. The Gita asks us to give up all possessions. This includes the possessions of charitable institutions also. For, if we go in for possessions in any form we have to commit all those wrongs which are accompanied with possession for private ends.

Harijan, 10-4-'49

8

NO MONEY DONATIONS

(*By Vinoba*)

I have been lately seized with a mania of running institutions on manual labour alone. I am convinced that without doing so our institutions can no longer function vigorously. It is not proper that after the passing away of Bapu people should still be asked to give money donations and we should carry on our work with the support of donated money. I hope that the Gandhi Memorial Fund will now be the last monetary fund collected in the name of Gandhiji. Hereafter none can and should collect any money in his name. Hereafter, we must build up labour; for, though people will be kind enough to give money for the sake of Gandhiji, it will spell our ruin.

Harijan, 5-1-'52

SECTION ELEVEN: TOWARDS VILLAGE SARVODAYA

1

THE PRINCIPLE OF SHARING

(*By K. G. Mashruwala*)

We must think of life as a whole and in all its varied aspects. Then there can be no watertight divisions and consequent clash of interests between agriculture and other industries or occupations. It should be possible for the worker of one occupation to take part in another occupation or have a share in the earnings of other occupations. A development on these lines should be aimed at.

The lack of entirety of outlook is the reason for the various kinds of injustices resulting from the existence of one person as the owner and another as the actual cultivator of land, standing in the relation of landlord and tenant, or owner and labourer or serf.

The landlord's share in what the tenant might produce with his labour has been long assumed to be legitimate; but the tenant gets no portion out of what the landlord might earn through other occupations, which he is enabled to pursue owing to the tenant relieving him from the labour on land.

It is sought to remove this injustice by abolishing the absentee landlord. He is asked either to become a pure agriculturist himself cultivating the land, or to cease to have any interest in that land. This does not seem to be the right direction of remedying the ill.

For the proper uplift of the Indian village it is important that a villager should not be merely an agriculturist, a herdsman or a trader. As a rule none of these occupations provides continuous engagement and full work during all the days of the year. Even if every one of these could be so developed as to provide full employment to persons engaged in it, it is necessary that they should also pursue a handicraft along with their main occupation. A mere agriculturist does not often develop fully on the intellectual plane. A mere shopkeeper or a mere artisan tends towards physical weakness and moral cowardice.

Village needs led to the rise of the artisan class ; where they could not be created locally, they were invited from other places. The same needs brought the mere agriculturist under the control of the trader. A few persons with greater intelligence or cunning than others of the agriculturist class also took to that profession. They did not require to abandon their lands. They were cultivated first through labourers and then through lessees.

Thus came about a division of labour. But in the division of earnings, the merchant claimed a share both in the produce of the land and the labour of the artisan, while he admitted nobody's share in the earnings of his trade. Similarly, the landlord claimed a share in the yield produced by the sweat of the labourer, and also exploited the skill of the artisan by giving him no more than just sufficient for bare existence, while he himself gave no share to the latter from his earnings from other lands or occupations. Thus the only person who worked hardest and got least was the land labourer and the artisan.

The reforms now attempted aim at eliminating the landlord and the 'middleman', (that is, the shopkeeper or the agent), making the artisan and the farm-labourer 'free' classes and enabling them to take a due share of the fruits of their labour.

Since none dares to stop large-scale industries, the industrialist retains a place of honour in the national economy.

The joint Hindu family system was based on blood relationship. There was a time when a family consisted of as many as 200 to 250 members. This made it possible to divide the work of cultivating land, tending the herds, manufacturing various articles, marketing produce etc. amongst its different members. All belonged to one family and consequently each one shared in the produce of all. But that system has now disappeared and it is not possible to revive it in the same form. But the principle of common sharing in the earnings of all which underlies that system is a valuable one. It can now be taken advantage of only through multi-purpose co-operative societies, and all laws and reforms should be devised with the object of promoting such societies.

The Tenancy Act also should pursue the same object. The so-called landlord, the agriculturist, the tenant, the farm-labourer, the village artisan, the shopkeeper and the emigrant, who goes abroad for a short while to earn, should all be so knitted together in a common society that every one shared the earnings of all others and none remained unemployed. Every one is of course to get a living wage. People should be guided and taught to a social and economic life based on such multi-purpose co-operative basis.

If the landlord is prepared to share all his other income with the tenant and the labourer, there could be no harm even if he retained the ownership of land.

There would be no objection to a trader investing his savings in the land and taking a share in its produce by getting it cultivated by labourers or tenants if he is equally prepared to share his other income with his tenants and labourers.

An enterprising young man in a joint Hindu family goes abroad and makes money. He has to share it with other members of the family, even as he himself gets a share in the earnings made at home during his absence. Why not extend the bounds of family, and include the tenant and the labourer, indeed, the whole village, in it? Then there should be no cause for jealousy. Rather, he would receive help and encouragement for his enterprises abroad. This is possible on the co-operative principle. When this happens the terms *absentee-landlord, unearned increment, exploitation* will fall out of use.

It is certainly more advantageous to cultivate larger farms of, say, 100 to 200 acres than those of 50 acres and similarly a bigger herd is more productive of wealth than a small one, provided always that this is done under the co-operative system.

If the new Tenancy Act is not favourable to the promotion of such co-operative societies, the defect should certainly be remedied in a suitable manner. The law must welcome and encourage erstwhile landlords to take greater interest in their lands, to go back to their villages and take to personal cultivation, improvement of agriculture and also promotion of industries in their villages, in such a way that the tenant, the artisan and the labourer all share together the joint earnings — all occupations and all earnings being regarded as joint.

The agriculturist is very much attached to his land and will not part with it easily. He will do his best to circumvent the law. It would, therefore, be much better for all if he could be induced to go the way of justice and Sarvodaya.

Harijan, 17-10-'48

2

VILLAGE MANAGEMENT

(*By Vinoba*)

Vinoba explained that the Government that was established in Delhi could not be expected to come to their village and deliver happiness to them. If their village was on fire the people from Hyderabad could not come to quench it. It was humanly impossible for a man or a group of men to sit at one place and look after the administration of such a big country. Vinobaji, therefore, impressed upon the people to have a committee of their own in every village to look after its affairs. This committee should study the requirements of the village and try to meet them as far as possible in the village itself. The committee should also free the people from the drink evil. They should also take care to see that quarrels, developed in towns and cities, like those of Congressmen and Socialists and other political groups, did not filter into their village. People might vote for any one they liked at the time of elections, but if outsiders came and tried to create political divisions in the village they must politely but definitely tell them that they had nothing to do with their political squabbles and opinions, and, so far as their affairs were concerned, they were neither Congressmen nor Socialists, nor Communists. They were all one group of Himayatnagarwalas, and nothing else. He warned them that politicians will go to them and instigate the poor against the rich, the employed against the employer, and one against another. They should tell the politicians that their village was one, that they were like one family and that they wanted to think about the problems of the village as others did about the problems of the country at large. If the villagers remained firm and did not allow the outside evils to enter into their village, they would be able to eliminate the evils of their village one by one.

Extract from his speech at village Himayatnagar in Hyderabad State

Harijan, 20-10-'51

3

EDUCATION FOR SARVODAYA

(*By Vinoba*)

A while ago when I was playing with the boys, the question arose in my mind whether the responsibility for bringing up these boys should rest on their respective parents or on the entire village. There was no difference between the son born to a rich man and the one born to a poor man. Both were equal manifestations of God and illumined their families equally well. If the village as a whole undertakes to look after its young children in the spirit of a parent to a child, the whole village would advance. That is the way to social progress and I place it before you for your consideration.

The children had no caste, continued Vinoba, nor knew distinctions of rich and poor. They were all equal creations of God. But the rich man attended to his own interests and neglected the wider interests of the village, and sent his boy to the city for education. The boy was urbanized and learnt to detest village life, and took permanent residence in the city. He could not be friends with the villagers and he did not work in the village. He only put in his appearance there at harvest time to get his share of the crop. But since he did not live in the village and did not attend to cultivation work, he failed to get as much as he should, and otherwise would. This led to ill-will between him and the villagers. And if the villagers combined against him he got alarmed and sought police-aid. He thought that the people had all turned Communists, and were out to harm him. The police had its own way of dealing with the situation. It was certainly not one of love. The strength of the police lay in the baton which they wielded. Ultimately it led the village to ruin and misery with the colossus of hatred stalking the countryside. So if the people wanted to build up a happy village, they must decide to provide for the education of the entire community of village children in the village itself.

When the boys of the village thus grew up together, Vinoba explained, they would also work jointly on the land. There would be neither fear nor ill-will. They would live in active amity with their friends and invite them to share their joys even as Krishna invited his cowherd companions to share his butter and curds. Such a village would grow into a Gokul, a veritable heaven on earth. For what was Gokul but the common sharing of the entire village wealth, whether it was milk and butter, or honey and sugar-cane or rice and Juar? When a man sat down for his meal all by himself like a thief, only the flies could flock on his food. But if he lovingly shared it with his friends, it would taste sweeter. One can love one's friends, but one cannot love the flies. His instinct of love therefore remained unsatisfied. And, he was led to do many awkward things. He kept dogs and cats as pets and tried in vain to bestow his unfilled love on them. Thus the problem grew more and more complicated, once people strayed from the right path. It was obvious that it could be straightened and resolved only by practising the art of common living: common reading and writing and studying at a common school.

Vinoba then went on to explain the sort of school which he envisaged for the village. He said that in the school which he would set up, everyone would be required to work. Teachers and pupils would apply themselves willingly to some sort of productive labour and through work they would learn whatever was useful for them. At present the boys of the well-to-do parents who went to school lost their capacity for work. This was the reverse of education, because it resulted in the diminution of one's innate capacities. Therefore Gandhiji had said that our schools should hum with all manner of useful activities. The boys should plough fields, spin yarn and weave it into cloth. And along with work and through it they should also learn. Rich boys and poor boys, Brahmana boys and Harijan boys should all work together in school and learn together. Such a school would lay the foundation for a new society free from social and economic inequality.

From his speech in Telangana, April 26, 1951

***Harijan*, 2-2-'52**

Education was expected to do two things. The training which students received should make them efficient enough to give the benefit of their education to the people. They should be able to return ten-fold what they had received. Education was like the operation of sowing a seed. A good seed and a proper sowing resulted in yielding several times more seeds. So should education do. It must repay several times the cost and labour expended upon it. This was the first thing which education was expected to yield.

The second thing expected of education was that it should provide all the food which a student needed for his development at his age. It should help to develop the capacities which lay hidden in his mind. Wise men had told them that the principal truth which they had to learn was that they were distinct from the body, the mind and the intellect. If education does not teach this, it is meaningless, because it fails in its main purpose. The central aim which education should address itself to is to enable the student to observe whether he is really progressing, that is, whether he is really developing all the noble potentialities which are man's heritage and whether he recognizes himself as distinct from the material environs and his corporal instrument, and whether he can exercise his will over them. In the Upanishads we find that a student was not regarded as a Snataka (graduate) even after he had acquired all the learning unless he had actually fulfilled the aims of education in terms of being and inner development. Not only had he to be a master of letters, but a master also of the will. He should be able to successfully observe his Vratas (pledged intentions) as an evidence of his mastery over himself. Like an able rider, he should be able to have full control over his body, sense and mind. The mastery over oneself, self-discipline and the proper use of the powers of the self — this is the greatest art, and should form the most important object of education. He who acquires it is a Vrata-Snataka (graduate in self-regulation), the master of academic learning being only a Vidya-Snataka (graduate in learning).

A student who has successfully passed this test proves to be really qualified for the effective service of his people. He alone becomes a good citizen and wherever he goes and whatever jobs he undertakes, he does so with confidence and courage. Today we find that a student, the moment he leaves the portals of the college, finds himself engulfed in the gloom of darkness. He might succeed in fixing himself somewhere, but he fails to find the work which really suits his liking and for which he is naturally equipped, nor does he get anywhere near the goal which he had set for himself. Circumstances toss him about and he crashlands somewhere. It is all a game of chance. But the Vrata-Snataka, the student who has been successful in the Vratas (self-regulations) secures mastery over the self, and acquires training in the arts of practical life, in agriculture and weaving etc., will not enter the world with his head stooping downwards like a crest-fallen wretch, but will march forward with open chest, and his heart full of the ardour born of self-confidence.

This does not mean that he would be haughty and insolent. Humility will also be his, because one who really acquires knowledge realizes that knowledge is limitless and that he has got only an infinitesimal part of it.

But along with humility, he will also have determination, self-confidence, fortitude, fearlessness etc. That is to say he must have Dhriti (holding power) along with Buddhi (intelligence), so that he will enter life like a virtuous hero. This self-confidence is expected to develop through education. If he possesses it, he will be able to serve the world. He will not feel life to be a burden. He will feel perfectly satisfied with what he learns. Learning, like eating, produces immediate satisfaction. As soon as you begin to eat you begin to feel happy. Happiness is not deferred to a period of even 2 or 3 days. So, too, is the case with knowledge. As soon as a person begins to feel that he has really learnt something, his face brightens up and his appetite for it increases. He does not feel that his time is wasted. He does not look to the day when his studies will be over, and he will be able to bid goodbye to his studies. Really, once a person had tasted of the spring of knowledge, he should always be seeking more of it continuously and till the end of his life. The Upanishads tell the student that after his student life is over, he should continue to increase his knowledge in the Grihasthashrama (the life of the householder). The Grihastha (householder) was a step in advance of the Brahmachari (student). The Grihastha who always increased his knowledge would be not only rendering what service he could directly, but would contribute towards making society righteous. He would have a sacred place in his house, where he would be studying regularly. Thus the Upanishads clearly contemplate the continuation of study after the regular training period was over. Acquisition of knowledge must continue till the end of life. He who had once tasted of the spring of knowledge could never think of giving it up, Shri Vinoba continued. The Upanishadic Rishi had linked the duty to learn and teach (स्वाध्याय प्रवचने च) along with every other duty and virtue. Thus he did not counsel merely righteousness (rita), truthfulness (satya), self-discipline (tapas) but enjoined, " Be righteous and learn and teach," " Be truthful, and learn and teach," " Practise self-discipline, and learn and teach," " Serve the world, and learn and teach," " Keep the sacrificial fire, and learn and teach," and so on. The gist of it was that the householder was expected to carry further the mission of knowledge throughout his life.

We have won independence and many responsibilities have devolved on us in its wake. They can be discharged satisfactorily, only if we have experts in every branch of knowledge. Our country will progress only if we continue to exert ourselves and take great pains in exploring the various branches of knowledge. But I see very few pains-taking and hardworking scholars. The main reason for this state of affairs is the modern system of education. For, when a pupil spends some five years in its routine, he loses all interest and becomes dry. His physical strength diminishes, his mental faculties become stunted, his sense organs are weakened and the worst of it all, he loses all vitality. He has not even an inkling of the soul, far less its distinctness from the body. And when he does not know how to keep his senses under his control, of what worth is his education ?

From his speech at Secunderabad.
Harijan, 14-7-'51

4

ADULT EDUCATION

(*By Vinoba*)

In every village there should be a regular reading of instructive literature. Just as we need food every day in order to live, so too, the mind must receive its food. While bread is the food for the body, knowledge is the food for the mind. Villagers should organize the reading of Tulsi Ramayana, the *Autobiography* of Gandhiji and *Gita Pravachan* (Vinoba's lectures on Gita). The peasant works the whole day and has no time to read for himself. If he reads, his eyes get affected. Hence every village should organize public reading. If they cultivate the habit of listening to good things their village will change in no time.

***Harijan*, 2-2-'52**

5

OUTLINE OF SARVODAYA

(*By Vinoba*)

Friends desired Vinoba to give them an outline of Sarvodaya. He said :

The villages of India must become self-supporting and they must be saved from fluctuations as much as possible. They must manufacture the finished goods which they require, in their own villages if the requisite raw material for them is produced locally. Machines should belong to society at large. There should be no intervening agency between production and ultimate distribution. A society based on Ahimsa cannot function through intermediate agencies. To bring about such a society village industries should thrive. All should get food and all must work. The economy of the nation should be planned on the lines of a joint family. If the Charkha can provide employment to all it should be used. If you cannot plan for the whole nation but have to discriminate, posing myself as a Communist, I say, in that case, you should discriminate in favour of the poor in making your plan. This is my outline of Sarvodaya in brief.

Harijan, 2-8-'52

6

TOWARDS ARTHIK SAMATA

(*By J. C. Kumarappa*)

Land should be given on probation, say for a period of ten years, to the cultivator. The contract might be renewed in the light of the agricultural efficiency displayed by the agriculturist in the past; the size of land given to a cultivator may be reduced or increased at the end of the period for a fresh period of ten years. Land given up by all those who were cultivators before will go back to the village community and it is the community which will give land to fresh entrants. The cropping plan will be framed by the village community after consulting the individual cultivators at the bottom and the District, State and Central Government at the top, and every individual cultivator will have to fall in line with the village community's plan. There will be a balanced cultivation taking into consideration the natural resources and the essential needs of the people. Self-sufficiency in essential commodities for a region of say 15 to 20 villages will be the aim, and only the surpluses will be sold through a multi-purpose co-operative society. The co-operative society will also determine cost of production of different commodities taking into consideration the man-hours required to produce a standard unit of a thing. Barter on the basis of exchange ratios based on these costs will be undertaken between individuals in the village through this co-operative society. All exports from and imports in the village and the region will be undertaken only through the multi-purpose co-operative society. The society will not be essentially a financial body, but it will be a functional co-operative organization, encouraging people to do the various industries and processes in an industry and arranging for the sales and purchases of different products. Manures will be produced ; village soil will be conserved by erecting bunds ; nullahs, rivers will be bunded so as to irrigate land ; internal roads will be made with the enthusiasm of the villagers, the Government only bearing the cost of materials. We must organize landless labour and educate them in their rights and obligations.

In regard to Swadeshi, we should again resurrect the old idea of Swadeshi, bearing in mind that by Swadeshi we mean, firstly, things produced in our vicinity and then only distant mill-made products. Foreign products, as far as possible, should not be purchased by the people. This is the passive part of Swadeshi. The active part of it lies in all persons applying their brains to the production of things as a substitute for foreign materials. After sufficient propaganda, a stage may come for active programmes — say bonfire of foreign goods etc. But it must be preceded by wide propaganda and action regarding both the aspects of Swadeshi by thousands of persons. Thus when we have redistribution of land and the Swadeshi spirit, we shall have full employment and an equitable redistribution of national dividend, and thus we shall attain Arthik Samata.

From lectures delivered at a camp at Seldoh, Madhya Pradesh.

Harijan, 24-1-'53

7

SARVODAYA PLANNING

(By K. G. Mashruwala)

Let us lay down the fundamental principles of the Sarvodaya approach to the problem of India's development:

(1) Respect for life is the first principle of Sarvodaya. The development of India means, primarily, healthy and all-round development of the life and personality of India's living beings, human as well as animal, the latter to the extent they have become a part and parcel of human life. The cow is the most important and symbolic of the socialized animals.

(2) The resources of Nature being an essential means for this purpose, their development cannot be neglected. But between life and Nature, the development of life should be the end, and that of Nature, the means for it. The latter should not be done by sacrificing life, nor should her resources be used extravagantly and wastefully. Even mute and inanimate Nature may not be 'exploited' in that sense. Although man is often influenced by his environment and becomes even a slave to it, nevertheless, ultimately, he is the master and maker of the environment and not its manufactured product; hence, the development of his personality cannot be subordinated to that of Nature. Nature has to be developed for him and with his aid; he is not to be made a mere tool for the development of Nature.

(3) Hence, the first concern of every society, as well as the State, should be to provide employment for every person within it, according to his capacity, with such work and means as are immediately available to it. The work and means should be improved progressively for him and with his aid to the extent necessary for the wellbeing of every one and only so far as such wellbeing is served.

(4) The standard of life should be distinguished from the standard of living; it is the former that is fundamental and not the latter; a rise in the standard of living might even lower the standard of life, by reducing man's

physical, moral, intellectual and spiritual standards, powers and potentialities. Hence, the progressive development of Nature must be consistent with rise in the standard of life, and not of living.

(5) Planning must proceed with two objects: Removal of natural or man-made impediments in the road to the development of man, and provision of means, training and guidance for it.

(6) The obstacles in the way of his development are: (i) Too much centralization of government and of production of wealth; (ii) the ownership and control by a few people, or by a machine-like corporation like the Government or a company, of land which they do not cultivate themselves, leading to absentee landlordism; (iii) money-dominated economy, leading to working for trade, commerce, profits, revenue etc. instead of for providing for the needs of oneself and society; this further leading to the creation of a large body of parasites; (iv) the institution of slavery in its modern forms; (v) the institution of interest, along with rights of proprietorship over large units of wealth to money-lenders and non-cultivators (in case of land) and to non-artisans (in case of industries); (vi) on the one hand, the absolute neglect of the common man's health and training, implements, seeds, raw materials by the State as well as by the advanced sections of society; and on the other, enforcement of rights and traditions, inculcation of customs, habits, vices, fashions, and luxuries, and provision of temptations, all bound to lead to his progressive deterioration from generation to generation; and (vii) institution of a political, economic and social order, in which he can play practically no part, take no initiative, but finds himself thoroughly tied down on all sides.

(7) Unless there are other nations available for unrestrained exploitation, no amount of the development of natural resources without the removal of these hindrances will bring about the welfare of even a majority, not to say every one — particularly in fully populated countries. The

problems of unemployment and high prices and hence of sub-human conditions of living, disease, poverty, hunger, slavery of the masses, unsafe and disgraceful conditions for women, dacoities, robberies, and corruption in administration and trade are bound to remain, and may even increase. There might be plenty of goods, even plenty of food, and yet there will be all the evils of insufficiency, unsatisfied needs, and want of scope for the play of one's abilities.

(8) Even if the Government planned nothing beyond the removal of these obstacles as rapidly as possible, the people would prosper, if not rapidly, at least slowly. If the plan seeks to go further to provide positive aids to the people, the immediate objectives should be : (i) To be thoroughly self-sufficient — I would say over-full — in respect of food and nutrition. On our self-sufficiency in nutrition will ultimately rest our Purna Swaraj, and not on our armaments. Hence, it must have priority over every other item of planning ; (ii) the food should not only be abundant, but should be normally available to every one without too much need for transportation. This means that there should be as many self-sufficient units as possible, the normal unit being the village ; (iii) it should also be normally available to every able-bodied person in an honourable manner, and not by way of charity, dole etc. This means that there should be no unemployment for any able-bodied person. Provision for employment of every one should be a joint item with production of food on a self-sufficiency basis ; (iv) the next positive item in planning would naturally have to be the training of the nation, and there can be no other system of training for a nation, with the above objective, except on the principles of Nai Talim, of which Basic Education is a part ; (v) provision of clean water both for irrigation and drinking, sanitation, hygiene etc. should precede doctoring and dispensing of drugs, vaccinations, injections etc. ; (vi) agricultural implements should be made available without creating indebtedness ; (vii) public utility services (post, telegraph, transport, loan of tractors, supply of seeds,

essentials like salt etc.), whether managed by Government or public corporations or private agencies, should not be administered for profit or in a way which will yield large balances ; (viii) temptations like liquor, intoxicating drugs, useless and expensive habits like those of tea, cold-drinks, tobacco, easy ways of making money, such as gambling, cross-word puzzles etc., vulgar shows, songs etc. should not be encouraged and licensed for revenue ; (ix) a Government which tells its people that it cannot establish a Welfare State unless the population is reduced, and plans for providing artificial means of birth-control, is as incompetent to govern as one that forces increase of population for imperialistic and war purposes. A training that incapacitates man from getting mastery over his passion and advises him to avoid the consequences of indulgence in it by questionable means is a failure of education as well as administration. Hence, the plan for education must be thoroughly overhauled.

These are a few of the basic objectives of Sarvodaya Planning, as I understand them. All planning, short-term or long-term, must be directed towards the achievement of these ends.

Harijan, 27-10-'51

SECTION TWELVE: WORK PROGRAMME

1

FIVE-FOLD PROGRAMME

(*By K. G. Mashruwala*)

From the two reviews published with this and the oral accounts of some of the vistors returning from the Conference, it appears that Vinobaji and other leaders of constructive work have placed a five-fold programme of work before the nation. Vinoba has tersely summed it up in one half of a verse as follows :

अन्तःशुद्धिः बहिःशुद्धिः श्रमः शान्तिः समर्पणम् ।

(Internal purity, external cleanliness, labcur, peace and dedication).

1. Antah-Shuddhi (internal purity) stands for the Shuddha-Vyavahara (honest-life) movement. It is a call to the people to renounce unfair ways of earning wealth or securing commodities and comforts, and to work together for that purpose.

2. Bahih-Shuddhi (external purity) is the Sarvodaya programme of cleanliness. We are generally credited with good sensitiveness for personal cleanliness. In the matter of public sanitation and cleanliness, even in those reputed for personal cleanliness, the sense is, at its best, just germinating. In the general public, it is very deficient and is the main cause of a good deal of disease and constant outburst of epidemics among the people. An intense drive for external cleanliness, personal as well as public, is another factor, needed for creating Sarvodaya.

3. Shrama (physical labour) is the third great condition for Sarvodaya. For centuries past we have done everything to destroy the dignity and value of labour and, not merely neglected, but suppressed and humiliated those who have, generation after generation, worked hard to

produce for us food, clothes, houses, furniture, ornaments and various comforts of life. Those who have washed our clothes and utensils, swept our streets and cowsheds, cleaned our latrines and urinals, manufactured our cloth, pots, shoes etc. stand lowest in our conception of dignity. We think of them with disrespect, behave towards them with insolence, and humiliate them in society; even in temples where we gather for worshipping our Creator, they have either no place or have a low and distant place. All honour is assigned to wealth, power and book-learning. The result is that production has diminished, the desire for a life of luxury and self-indulgence has increased, and while no one wants to labour, everybody seeks to get comfort which hard labour can produce. This is an impossible aim. Whether we labour with our bare hands or with the assistance of implements or machines, labour we must. The capacity and will to labour must be regarded as the mark of a developed body and cultured mind.

4. Shanti (establishment of peace) is the fourth item. Peace is not to be understood here in its restricted context of abolition of war. Abolition of war is not ruled out, but war is magnified edition of small conflicts which take place frequently in every small group. If small groups know how to live in amity, to resolve petty disputes, and to abolish fear and jealousy from their small world, it will cut at the root of war in the larger world.

5. The last item is Samarpana, that is dedication of one hank of self-spun yarn on Gandhiji's annual day. This small hank of self-spun yarn is symbolical of the dedicator's respect for Gandhiji, faith in the Sarvodaya ideal, faith in personal service, faith in the performance of physical labour, faith in a non-violent and non-exploiting order, and of the equal status of the rich and the poor.

Harijan, 28-4-'51

2

SAMAGRA SEVA

(*By Vinoba*)

Vinoba said that Samagra Seva (all-round service) did not mean tackling all things simultaneously. It meant that round about a selected item should grow and develop other items of work gradually and naturally.

Explaining his point further, Vinoba recalled his visit, many years ago, to Anantpur (M. P.) where a certain worker had a Khadi centre. The work there had come to a stop, and Vinoba was asked to investigate into the causes. Vinoba examined the work carefully and pointed out that one of the reasons why the work had ceased to grow was that the worker had concentrated exclusively on Khadi, to the utter neglect of all other details of life. For instance, the villagers eased themselves in the open, and yet the glaring indecency had not attracted his notice. He was fully occupied with Khadi work, and had no eye for anything else. Vinoba said that that was an instance of exclusive concentration which was opposed to all-round vigilance. Indeed it was not concentration, but a sort of narrow polarized vision. While narrowness was not desirable, it did not mean that they could dispense with concentration. Both concentration and an all-embracing outlook were necessary.

From the summary of his speech.

***Harijan*, 23-6-'51**

3

BOYCOTT AS PART OF CONSTRUCTIVE WORK

(*By Dhirendra Mazumdar*)

Those who have the ambition of working for a really new social order must realize that while they do something constructive they must also simultaneously work to end the present social order. That is the necessary characteristic of a revolution.

Prerequisites of a Revolution

A revolution can be brought about either by the Government or by the masses of people and the public workers. If the Government wishes to initiate the process then it must inevitably stop machine-production, buffalo-protection and the old system of education. If the Government does not decide to do this, then all the money that it spends on the promotion of decentralized industries is sheer waste. If on the other hand this revolution has to be brought about by public organizations and public workers then they must adopt a double programme — promotion of Charkha, village industries, cow-protection and basic education on the one hand, and boycott of machine-production, of buffalo-rearing and of the old education on the other. They must in their own life and in the lives of their institutions adopt the boycott programme and take a vow to implement it. They must persuade other individuals and institutions to do the same. And when they find that the public is sufficiently aroused they should initiate a comprehensive movement of boycott. If we fail to do this our constructive work will be sheer waste in terms of a social revolution.

In the course of my tour whenever I have presented this idea to my co-workers or to directors of institutions, I have met with ready approval. There has been no disagreement in principle. All have agreed that this is the right thing to do. But they all speak of great difficulties in the way of implementing the programme. They say that the circumstances are not favourable. If that is so why do our workers and institutions feel dissatisfied when the Government pleads inability to restrict machine-production? Since the Government too has to face the same difficulties we should have no grievance against it. We talk of revolution, and yet we are cowed down by adverse circumstances and by difficulties. We should not then be surprised at the attitude the Government takes.

I do not deny that there are occasions when circumstances prove too forbidding. But can we honestly say that our workers and institutions have done all that they could do, and that it is only the circumstances that thwart their efforts? I do not think this is so.

What is needed is clear vision, determination and dedication. To begin with, we should raise the cry of boycott of machine-production in the sphere of food and clothing first. Later on we may extend our cry to other spheres. We may also pick out specific items and concentrate on them. All individuals and institutions may not be equally effective but the progress will be maintained. But if we fail to make conscious effort in this direction we shall soon find ourselves without goal and doomed to failure. Our sacrifice and character may bring us individual spiritual consolation and contentment, but the great dream of a social revolution will remain unfulfilled.

We have seen that in the great days of the Swaraj struggle our movement for Swadeshi would have come to nought if we had not simultaneously carried on the boycott movement against Videshi (foreign goods). Similarly now if we fail to start a boycott movement against machine-production along with a movement for popularizing village industries etc., all our cry for village industries will not do more than give a little help to some needy people. It certainly cannot create a social order, decentralized and self-sufficient, and free from exploitation.

I do hope that my co-workers and the constructive institutions will give serious thought to this appeal of mine.

Harijan, 13-10-'51

APPENDIX

THE PARABLE

[The following is the parable of Jesus which inspired Ruskin to choose *Unto This Last* as the title of his book and which Gandhiji translated into *Sarvodaya* to indicate his teaching. — Ed.]

For the kingdom of heaven is like unto a man that is an householder, which went out early in the morning to hire labourers into his vineyard.

And when he had agreed with the labourers for a penny a day, he sent them into his vineyard.

And he went out about the third hour, and saw others standing idle in the market place.

And said unto them: Go ye also into the vineyard, and whatsoever is right, I will give you. And they went their way.

Again he went out about the sixth and ninth hour, and did likewise.

And about the eleventh hour he went out, and found others standing idle, and said unto them: Why stand ye here all the day idle?

They say unto him: Because no man hath hired us. He saith unto them. Go ye also into the vineyard; and whatsoever is right, that shall ye receive.

So when even was come, the lord of the vineyard saith unto his steward, Call the labourers, and give them their hire, beginning from the last unto the first.

And when they came that were hired about the eleventh hour, they received every man a penny.

But when the first came, they supposed that they should have received more; and they likewise received every man a penny.

And when they had received it, they murmured against the good man of the house.

Saying, These last have wrought but one hour, and thou hast made them equal unto us, which have borne the burden and heat of the day.

But he answered one of them, and said, Friend, I do thee no wrong : Didst not thou agree with me for a penny ?

Take that thine is, and go thy way : I will give unto this last even as unto thee.

Matthew, XX, 1-14

NON-ENGLISH WORDS WITH THEIR MEANINGS

Adharmic — contrary to Dharma or duty ; hence evil
Ahimsa — non-violence ; love
Akhada — physical culture institute
Arthik Samata — economic equality
Avatar — incarnation
Bapu — lit. father ; a term of affection used for Gandhiji
Bhangi — scavenger
Bigha — 3,025 square yards of land
Bhoodan — land gift
Bidi — country cigarette
Brahmacharya — chastity ; continence
Chapati — flat, unleavened bread
Charkha — spinning wheel
Crore — 10 million
Dal — pulse
Daridranarayana — God in the form of the poor
Dharma — duty ; religion
Dhurna — picketing by squatting in one's way
Divali — the festival of lights
Ezhava — an 'untouchable' caste of Malabar
Fakir — religious mendicant
Gadi — throne ; seat of honour
Ganja — flower of Indian hemp which has an intoxicating effect when smoked with tobacco
Go Seva — work for the welfare of cattle
Gramodyoga — village industries
Gur — jaggery ; unrefined brown product derived from palm juice or sugar cane juice and used for sweetening like sugar
Harijan — lit. people of God, as Gandhiji called 'untouchables'
Hartal — temporary cessation of business or work
Himsa — violence

Holi — Spring festival
Jagirdar — holder of rent-free land
Juar — Indian maize
Kali — Goddess of darkness and destruction
Kanyadan — giving away the daughter in marriage
Khaddar, Khadi — handspun, hand-woven cloth
Kisan — peasant
Lakh — 100,000
Lathi — long bamboo stick
Mandal — club
Mandir — temple
Mantra — slogan ; formula
Math — monastry ; hermitage
Mela — fair ; assembly
Mohalla — section of a village or town
Moksha — liberation ; salvation ; self-realization
Moplah — a sect of Muslims in Malabar
Nai-Talim — lit. New Education, i.e. Pre-basic, Basic and Post-Basic Education
Nullah — rivulet
Panchayat — a council of five members or more
Pariah — 'untouchable'
Prabhat-pheri — morning procession
Purna — full ; complete
Ramanama — lit. name of Rama, or God
Ramanavami — the birth anniversary of Rama
Ramarajya — Kingdom of God ; the ideal social order
Razinama — deed of agreement
Rishi — seer
Ryot — peasant
Safai — sanitation
Samaj — association
Samagra Seva — all-round service
Samiti — committee
Sampatti — wealth
Sampatti-dan — giving of wealth for charity
Samya-yoga — ideal of equality
Sanatani — orthodox ; one who follows the ancient faith
Sangh — association

Satyagraha — non-violent resistance; lit. clinging to truth
Satyagrahi — non-violent resister of evil; lit. one who clings to truth
Sevak — public worker
Shanti Dal — Peace Brigade
Shikar — hunt
Smriti — tradition
Svadharma — one's duty in the light of one's place in society
Swadeshi — the duty to serve one's neighbours and therefore to use only articles produced by them
Swaraj — self-government
Tahsil — a part of an administrative district
Tahsildar — officer in charge of a tahsil
Vaid — doctor of Indian medicine
Vakil — lawyer
Van Mahotsava — tree-planting festival
Varna — caste
Varnashrama — social grouping based on pursuit of hereditary occupations
Yajna — sacrifice offered to the Deity
Yatra — pilgrimage
Zamindar — landlord

INDEX